CONFLICTING SIGNS

CONFUSE SINNERS

# CONFLICTING SIGNS

# CONFUSE SINNERS

## DO YOU GIVE CLEAR DIRECTIONS?

TRENT THOMPSON
PAUL MORSE

© 2011 by Trent Thompson and Paul Morse. All rights reserved.
2nd Printing 2014.

© 2011 Interior illustrations by Ron Wheeler.

Trusted Books is an imprint of Deep River Books. The views expressed or implied in this work are those of the author. To learn more about Deep River Books, go online to www.DeepRiverBooks.com.

No part of this publication may be reproduced, stored in a retrieval system or transmitted in any way by any means—electronic, mechanical, photocopy, recording or otherwise—without the prior permission of the Publisher, except as provided by USA copyright law.

All Scriptures are taken from the *King James Version* of the Bible.

ISBN 13: 978-1-63269-282-5
Library of Congress Catalog Card Number: 2009911320

# CONTENTS

Acknowledgments.............................. vii

Salvation Quiz................................. ix

Introduction .................................xiii

Preface.......................................xix

**Part 1: Wrong Routes to Salvation**
1. Repent of Your Sins ....................... 1
2. Confess Your Sins ....................... 11
3. Give Up Your Bad Habits................. 15
4. Be Convicted of Your Sins ................ 21
5. Sorrow for Your Sins ..................... 25
6. Give Your Heart to Jesus ................. 31
7. Live It or Lose It ....................... 35
8. Keep the Faith .......................... 45
9. Make a Public Profession of Faith........... 53

10. Pray Through. . . . . . . . . . . . . . . . . . . . . . . . . 57
11. Make Jesus Lord of Your Life. . . . . . . . . . . . . . 61
12. Say the Sinner's Prayer. . . . . . . . . . . . . . . . . . . 77

**Part 2: The One Way to Salvation**
13. Understanding Salvation . . . . . . . . . . . . . . . . . 83
14. One Way to Heaven. . . . . . . . . . . . . . . . . . . . . 93
15. Assurance of Salvation. . . . . . . . . . . . . . . . . . 101

**Part 3: Winning Others To Christ**
16. Pray for Power. . . . . . . . . . . . . . . . . . . . . . . . 109
17. Motivation for Soul-Winning . . . . . . . . . . . . . 113
18. Door-to-Door Evangelism . . . . . . . . . . . . . . . 119
19. Altar Salvations . . . . . . . . . . . . . . . . . . . . . . . 127
20. Handing Out Tracts . . . . . . . . . . . . . . . . . . . . 131
21. Other Methods of Witnessing . . . . . . . . . . . . 137
22. Presenting the Plan of Salvation . . . . . . . . . . 143

**Part 4: Staying the Course**
23. Fruit Inspection. . . . . . . . . . . . . . . . . . . . . . . 151
24. Discipleship. . . . . . . . . . . . . . . . . . . . . . . . . . 161
25. The Burning Building . . . . . . . . . . . . . . . . . . 165
26. What Are You Going to Do? . . . . . . . . . . . . . 169

Study Guide. . . . . . . . . . . . . . . . . . . . . . . . . . . . . . 173

Notes . . . . . . . . . . . . . . . . . . . . . . . . . . . . . . . . . . . 191

Glossary . . . . . . . . . . . . . . . . . . . . . . . . . . . . . . . . 193

# ACKNOWLEDGMENTS

I (PAUL) WOULD like to thank Rev. Thayne Bodenmiller, Ruth Cade, Rita Bostick, Rev. Gary Henry, Suzy Lange, Susan Allen, and Linda Sanders for reviewing the manuscript. I would also like to thank Pastor Willie Elmore and Lola Blanchard for sharing their thoughts on salvation. I would especially like to thank my mother, Olive Morse, for asking a key question which resulted in the addition of the preface giving the book a much clearer focus.

# SALVATION QUIZ

CAN YOU GIVE clear directions about salvation? Find out by taking the quiz below.

**Directions:** Circle T for True and F for False for each of the following statements.

T/F  1. In order to receive salvation, a person must first turn from his or her sins.

T/F  2. A person must confess his or her sins to get saved.

T/F  3. You cannot be saved unless you make Jesus Lord of your life.

T/F  4. Reciting a sinner's prayer will save a person.

T/F  5. A drug addict must give up drugs in order to get saved.

T/F  6. A person who did not turn completely from his or her sins must never have really gotten saved.

# CONFLICTING SIGNS CONFUSE SINNERS

T/F 7. Unless you keep your life clean, you will lose your salvation.

T/F 8. A person cannot be saved unless he or she goes through a period of conviction and is ready to receive salvation.

T/F 9. Committing one's life to Christ is an essential part of obtaining salvation.

T/F 10. Unless a person feels genuine sorrow for his or her sins, he or she cannot be saved.

The answers are on the following page.

## SALVATION QUIZ

## Answers to the Salvation Quiz:

1. False
2. False
3. False
4. False
5. False
6. False
7. False
8. False
9. False
10. False

How well did you score? Don't feel bad if you didn't do well, because we designed the quiz to highlight many of the common misconceptions about salvation. If you answered true for any of the questions, this book is for you. Read on as we try to answer these questions: How do you get saved, and how do you lead someone to Christ?

# INTRODUCTION

HAVE YOU EVER heard anyone discuss the importance of turning from your sins or sorrowing for your sins as a prerequisite for salvation? Many people believe that you cannot be saved unless you make Jesus Lord of your life. Many fundamentalists and evangelicals easily dismiss requirements for salvation such as baptism or church membership as being unscriptural, while many add one or more requirements to salvation that are more subtle but equally unscriptural. As you will see, these beliefs are no more a part of obtaining salvation than church membership is.

## Our Purpose

This book is not about the provision of salvation as taught by most Baptist and Protestant denominations, which is as follows: Jesus Christ, God's sinless Son, died in the sinner's place to pay his sin debt. He took the sinner's place at Calvary. He arose from the dead after three days, signifying His victory over death, hell, and the grave.

## CONFLICTING SIGNS CONFUSE SINNERS

The problem with teaching on salvation does not lie with its provision, but with its misapplications. This book is intended to answer the question: How does a person get saved? In other words, what is man's part in receiving salvation from Christ? This may seem like a simple question, but if you ask even just a few Christians for an answer, you are likely to get widely varying responses. This is because many true believers presume their own experiences are the measure of what is necessary to receive salvation and thus promote false ideas about salvation. This does not mean that they are not saved; it only means they do not fully understand the application of salvation. You also might have had some of the same experiences when you were saved. The fact that they are unessential doesn't mean that you are unsaved; it only means that you need to put your own experience in proper perspective.

If you listen carefully to your pastor, Sunday school teacher, evangelists, and guest speakers, you will discover that they differ on numerous points of doctrine. Many of these points are minor. However, some of them may involve serious errors. If you believe everything you are taught, then you are like those mentioned in Ephesians 4:14: "That we henceforth be no more children, tossed to and fro, and carried about with every wind of doctrine, by the sleight of men, and cunning craftiness, whereby they lie in wait to deceive." Rather, we should be like those mentioned in Acts 17:11: "These were more noble than those in Thessalonica, in that they received the word with all readiness of mind, and searched the scriptures daily, whether those things were so."

Are you ready to search the scriptures? What does the Bible say? Lets accept it and believe it!

One of Satan's most powerful and subtle weapons is that of confusion. What better way to keep people from getting saved than to allow the doctrine of salvation to

## INTRODUCTION

become corrupted? It is our prayer that this book will give you a clearer understanding of what is essential to obtain salvation and what it is not, thus enhancing your ability to more effectively win souls to Christ.

Not only must we work at clearly presenting the plan of salvation to the unsaved, but we must also point out and correct misconceptions whenever we hear anyone adding nonessentials to the plan of salvation. "Beloved, when I gave all diligence to write unto you of the common salvation, it was needful for me to write unto you, and exhort you that ye should earnestly contend for the faith which was once delivered unto the saints" (Jude 3). God holds all of us accountable for our efforts to spread the gospel, to grow spiritually, and to be devoted to the study and understanding of His Word.

## Outline of Book

The preface is comprised of stories about salvation experiences that describe how sinners and saints alike have become confused by gospel presentations. We devote the first section of this book entirely to describing and refuting incorrect doctrines and methods of salvation. The second section will give the reader a better understanding of salvation as we discuss the correct application of salvation and related topics, such as the assurance of salvation and eternal security. In the third section we look at methods of soul-winning and their effectiveness. The final section of the book covers fruit inspection and discipleship.

## Use of Humor

There are many comments, analogies, illustrations, and dialogs throughout the book that are quite humorous (at least in the opinion of the authors). We are in no way poking fun at the many sincere Christians, teachers, pastors, and theologians who have been taught or teach many of the variations on doctrine that we dispute in this volume. We used humor only to make the book more enjoyable and to help get certain points across.

Please do not let the humor stand in the way of your receiving the book's message. It is not intended to offend. If you stop reading because you become offended, then you will miss the book's message.

## Doctrinal Statement

The authors believe the Bible is the inspired Word of God and that the Holy Scriptures are the only basis of doctrine for Christians. We believe that Bible words are defined by their Bible usage. We do not build Bible doctrine on what the Bible doesn't say. We also do not base our beliefs on what people teach or preach, because the Bible is the final authority on all doctrinal issues.

## A Final Note

You have probably heard of turning from sins, making Jesus Lord of one's life, and the "sinner's prayer." Other ideas in this book may be less familiar. It is important to realize that your familiarity with incorrect teachings on salvation is dependent on several factors. These include your denomination, the region of the country in which you live, the pastor of your church, the Bible school your pastor attended, and the era in which you grew up. You should also be aware that you might have heard some of these ideas worded differently or heard similar teachings with a somewhat different emphasis. Please realize the authors

# INTRODUCTION

have tried to address the topic of confusion over salvation in as broad a way as possible. If you find a chapter that addresses salvation in an unfamiliar way, we recommend you skip ahead to another chapter more in line with your experience.

We designed this book to guide you into a better understanding of the various aspects of salvation and motivate you to become a soul-winner. It is not about some trivial theological doctrine of little significance. Rather, it deals with the most important topic in the entire world: the salvation of lost souls.

# PREFACE
# SO WHAT'S THE BIG DEAL?

CONFLICTING SIGNS DO indeed confuse sinners. Wrong teaching on salvation causes some individuals to reject salvation, stunts the growth of those who have accepted it, and causes others to live in constant doubt and fear because they are never truly sure if they are saved. Some feel they must get "resaved," some receive false hope of heaven, and others give up on Christianity altogether because they decide that salvation doesn't work. The following stories about various salvation experiences are designed to illustrate the effects of this confusion about salvation in the lives of both unbelievers and believers alike.

> Do you give clear directions for salvation,
> or do the lost stay lost and become more confused?

## Marriage First, Salvation Second

My (Trent's) former pastor was out witnessing with a friend. The two were visiting in the home of a young couple, and the pastor explained the plan of salvation and offered an invitation for salvation. The man said, "We can't get saved; we're not married." When the pastor heard this, he abandoned the salvation invitation and started to discuss possible arrangements to get this couple married. This couple didn't get saved because of an incorrect understanding of salvation. They thought that because they weren't living right, they couldn't get saved—and the pastor agreed.

## Second Salvations

A misguided youth director convinced a group of church teens that they needed to get saved despite their previous professions of faith. The youth director felt this was necessary because the teens' lifestyles didn't line up with that of saved persons. His message that evening focused on rock music. He told the teens that if they listened to rock music and enjoyed it, they must not really be saved. Many of these teens went forward that evening to get "resaved."

Those teens were made to doubt their salvation because of their behavior. Now they will continue to doubt—or their doubts will reoccur—once there is a lapse in their behavior.

## Stunted Growth

The wrong beliefs of Christians can discourage new converts from growing in Christ. While out soul-winning one evening, we came across a man who didn't want to get saved. He said, "I've already been saved three times." He described how he had repented and asked Christ to save him. It seems that some relatives in his former church had told him that because he still had a problem with drinking, he must not really be saved. They told him that he really needed to repent of his sins so he could really be saved.

## PREFACE

After his third "repentance," this man decided that salvation didn't work.

What this man really needed was for someone to give him the assurance, by showing him from the Bible, that he truly was saved. After that, he needed help with his alcohol problem.

This man was made to doubt his salvation by well-meaning but ignorant believers who based their own assurance of salvation on their changed lives rather than on the written Word of God. As a result, this man now can't trust God to help him with his drinking problem because he's been led to wrongly believe that he doesn't even know God.

### Barriers of Unforgiveness

Before I (Trent) was saved, I confessed my sins to God and tried to get right with Him. One day, I went with a friend to a minister's house. The minister asked if I wanted to trust Christ. I told him Yes. After I prayed with him I didn't feel like anything happened. He asked if I was holding a grudge, and I said that I was holding one against a former employee. After that we prayed again, and this time I did feel like I was saved.

What would have happened if I had been unwilling to forgive someone and the topic had come up before I prayed to trust in Christ? My guess is that the minister would have told me that I couldn't get saved.

### No Gain, No Loss

Shortly after I (Trent) trusted Christ as my Savior at the age of twenty, my wife and I invited another couple to our home. My purpose in inviting this couple was to get an opportunity to witness to them. The husband had been one of the first people I had told when I trusted Christ as my Savior some months earlier, and at the time he had commented, "I probably need to do that." After dinner, I explained the plan of salvation and asked him if he would like to trust Christ. He replied that he would not, and he did not.

Later, I concluded that one of the barriers for getting him to trust Christ as his Savior was the influence of his mother's denomination on him, which held that people would lose their salvation if they sinned. I tried to put myself in his shoes, and this question came to mind: Why bother to get something that you can't keep past the next weekend?

## Your Beliefs Do Matter

You may wonder if it really matters whether or not a person has an incorrect understanding of repentance. People have become saved despite wrong teaching, and maybe some have been motivated to give up their sins before the Holy Spirit would have urged them to do so.

In fact, we have personal experience of a church where this teaching has had a dramatic effect. The church had an average attendance of 900 to 1,000, with 400 of these being children who were bused in every week. Between 75 and 100 people went soul-winning every week, and the number of reported salvations per year was around 1,500. The obvious question to ask is this: If 1,500 people become saved each year, then why is the attendance only 900 to 1,000—especially given the fact that 400 of those people are bused in?

One of the reasons for this problem is wrong teaching on repentance, which has led to a lack of discipleship in this

## PREFACE

church. Some of the members firmly believe that in order to get saved, a person must turn from his or her sins, and the church teaches that any person who is truly saved will show clear evidence that he or she has turned from those sins. That person will want to come to church, read his or her Bible, pray, and give up wrong behaviors like smoking and drinking.

Because of this belief that everything happens at salvation, the members of this church have not seen the need to disciple anyone. Consequently, many of the hundreds of people who were saved by the soul-winners in this church were only minimally discipled after they were brought into the congregation. The church just assumed that if these people were truly saved, the changes would have automatically taken place.

If you are a reasonably mature Christian, you know that you did not change your life on your own. It took many hours of teaching, prayer, Bible study, and the helping hands of many other Christians to disciple you. So, you can see that beliefs do matter. They do affect our methods of evangelism and discipleship.

## Perspectives Matter

Beliefs about salvation will also affect a person's responses and behaviors about who has actually become saved. One man who used to attend the church described above had this to say: "If all those kids who got saved had really gotten saved, this town would be a lot different." This man believed that the children who claimed to have received salvation didn't really get saved because there wasn't a change in their behavior. This man probably wouldn't count decisions made to trust Christ as others had, and he would probably place a bigger emphasis on the need to turn from one's sins in his salvation presentation.

| | |
|---|---|
| Traveler: | Excuse me. Could you give me directions to heaven? |
| Gas Station Attendant: | Oh that's easy; I drive by there every day. First, you turn left out here... I think. Then you go past two red lights—or is it three? Um, I'm not sure. Well, anyhow, on the left you'll see a drugstore. Turn right when you get to the water tower. Go five blocks and you'll be there. You can't miss it! |

## Selfish Motives

I (Trent) once visited a young man who had made a public profession of his faith at our church. When I talked with him, he said, "I thought I was saved before—this was my third time getting saved. The first two times I was saved, I believed for a selfish motive. When I surrendered my life, I really got saved. This was an unselfish motive."

I wonder if this young man's "selfish motive" was staying out of hell. I also wonder if surrendering his life was also a selfish motive. It has been our observation that people initially surrender only the areas of their lives in which they need help. This man was obviously confused about salvation, so I led him to assurance of his salvation.

How many other people doubt their salvation because they are confused by similar ideas?

# PREFACE

## No Pot Smoking Allowed

I (Trent) was out witnessing with a fellow church member one evening in a trailer park. When we knocked on the door of one gentleman's home, he invited us inside. We carefully explained the plan of salvation to him. As we were finishing, my partner noticed a marijuana cigarette lying on a table. When he asked about it, the man said, "Yes, I smoke marijuana." My partner then explained that until he gave it up, he couldn't get saved.

Would this man have trusted Christ if the soul-winner had not gotten distracted by his wrong belief? What if we hadn't seen the marijuana cigarette? What about the man's other sins? Would he have to give those up as well? This man wasn't given the opportunity to get saved because of the wrong belief of a soul-winner.

Conflicting signs have clearly confused both unbelievers and believers alike. In an effort to clear up some common misconceptions, in the next section we will highlight wrong routes to salvation and point the reader in the right direction: complete trust in Christ!

# PART 1

# WRONG ROUTES TO SALVATION

WRONG ROUTE #1

# REPENT OF YOUR SINS

REPENT OF YOUR sins. Make a U-turn. That's what many unbelievers hear they must do to receive salvation. But what does it mean to repent? Does it mean we stop sinning so we can get saved, or does it mean that once we're saved we will stop sinning? Maybe it means we need to be willing to give up sinning or that we agree to no longer pursue sin. Since we cannot define Bible words by what we think they mean let's look at passages where the word *repentance* is used.

## CONFLICTING SIGNS CONFUSE SINNERS

# How is Repentance Used in the Bible?

Let's start by taking a look at some New Testament verses:

In those days came John the Baptist, preaching in the wilderness of Judaea, And saying, *Repent* ye: for the kingdom of heaven is at hand.
(Matt. 3:12, author emphasis)

Now after that John was put in prison, Jesus came into Galilee, preaching the gospel of the kingdom of God, And saying, The time is fulfilled, and the kingdom of God is at hand: *repent* ye, and believe the gospel.
(Mark 1:14–15, author emphasis)

*Repent* ye therefore, and be converted, that your sins may be blotted out.
(Acts 3:19a, author emphasis)

As you can see from these passages repentance is essential to salvation, because it was preached by John the Baptist, Jesus, and Peter.

Salvation Comes First; It Makes
Turning from Sins Possible

## REPENT OF YOUR SINS

Most Christians believe that in each case repentance means turning from sin. If this is true we should be able to substitute *turning from sins* every time the word *repentance* is used. Here are five verses with *turning from sin* substituted for the word *repent* or *repentance*:

> From that time Jesus began to preach, and to say, *"Turn from your sins*: for the kingdom of heaven is at hand."
> (Matt. 4:17)

> And they went out, and preached that men should *turn from their sins*.
> (Mark 6:12)

> And he said, "Nay, father Abraham: but if one went unto them from the dead, they will *turn from their sins*."
> (Luke 16:30)

> And the times of this ignorance God winked at; but now commandeth all men everywhere to *turn from their sins*.
> (Acts 17:30)

> But showed first unto them of Damascus, and at Jerusalem, and throughout all the coasts of Judaea, and then to the Gentiles, that they should *turn from their sins* and turn to God, and do works meet for *turning from sins*.
> (Acts 26:20)

(Author's substitution throughout)

> Only a believer can turn from
> sins because an unbeliever doesn't
> have the means to turn from sins
> until he is born again of the Spirit
> and receives a new nature.

## CONFLICTING SIGNS CONFUSE SINNERS

Now let's take those same five verses and substitute *change their mind* for the word *repent* or *repentance*.

> From that time Jesus began to preach, and to say, "*Change your minds*: for the kingdom of heaven is at hand."
> (Matt. 4:17)

> And they went out, and preached that men should *change their minds*.
> (Mark 6:12)

> And he said, "Nay, father Abraham: but if one went unto them from the dead, they will *change their minds*."
> (Luke 16:30)

> And the times of this ignorance God winked at; but now commandeth all men everywhere to *change their minds*:
> (Acts 17:30)

> But showed first unto them of Damascus, and at Jerusalem, and throughout all the coasts of Judaea, and then to the Gentiles, that they should *change their minds* and turn to God, and do works meet for *changing their minds*.
> (Acts 26:20)

(Author's substitution throughout)

While these substitutions are a bit cumbersome it appears that both of them will work in these verses. The question is: Which one is right? While there are several meanings for words that are translated repent or repentance, *the Greek word used for repent in each of these verses means, "to change one's mind."* It does not mean to turn from sins. What do we need to change our minds about? We need to change our minds about what we are trusting in for salvation. Are we trusting in Christ's righteousness or our own righteousness? (see Rom. 10:2-3).

## True Salvation Repentance

Repentance is a means of preparing the way for complete trust to take place. Trusting without repenting is not trust; it is distrust.

John the Baptist preached repentance: "In those days came John the Baptist, preaching in the wilderness of Judaea, And saying, Repent ye: for the kingdom of heaven is at hand. For this is he that was spoken of by the prophet Esaias, saying, The voice of one crying in the wilderness, Prepare ye the way of the Lord, make his paths straight" (Matt. 3:1-3). Repentance prepares the way for the Lord. The Jews had to make a clean break. They had to begin repenting, that is, taking their belief or trust out of whatever it was in and start preparing to trust in Christ.

Which of the following equations is true?

Trust in Christ + turning from sin = salvation
Trust in Christ + reformation = salvation
Trust in Christ + baptism = salvation
Trust in Christ + church membership = salvation
Trust in Christ + sorrow for sins = salvation
Trust in Christ + conviction = salvation
Trust in Christ + surrendering your life = salvation
Trust in Christ - faith in good works = salvation
Trust in Christ - faith in reformation = salvation
Trust in Christ - faith in surrendering your life = salvation

The only equations that can be true for any individual are the last three. You cannot add anything to faith in Christ in order to get saved. In order to receive salvation, you must repent of the sin that conflicts with what it takes to be saved (complete trust in Christ). The only way to have complete faith in Christ is to give up your faith in whatever you believe in for salvation and trust Christ as your only hope for heaven.

If you go soul-winning and the prospect happens to be Catholic, you need to get her to repent. You may present the gospel, convince her to trust Christ, and lead her in a prayer where she tells Christ she is trusting Him. However, the potential convert may have actually meant: "Christ, I have a little trust left that is neither in the Church nor in its sacraments. I'm placing all my remaining trust in you." Did this person really get saved? Absolutely not, because she failed to repent of Catholicism which was the object of her trust. In order for anyone to completely trust Christ for salvation, they must give up their current object of trust for salvation.

> Turning from your sins
> doesn't pay the penalty for them.

If a man is willing to turn from all his sins but only partially trust Christ, he will die and go to hell. On the other hand, if a man is only willing to put his faith completely in Christ, he will be saved. The person who is willing to trust Christ as his only hope for heaven has done all the repenting necessary for his salvation.

What if a man is an alcoholic? Is it necessary for him to give up alcohol in order to get saved? No, he only needs to repent of the sin that conflicts with putting 100 percent faith in Christ. Since most folks aren't trusting and depending on alcohol either partially or completely to get them to heaven, that sin does not conflict with believing on Christ. But on the other hand, if someone told him that in order to get saved he must give up his alcohol, it has increased the chance that he will trust partially in his own ability to turn from alcohol and trust partially in Christ's death on the cross. If that is the case, he can't be saved. If it is not essential to turn from alcohol in order to be saved, then it shouldn't be included in the plan of salvation.

> Jesus doesn't accept the sinner on the basis of his turning from his sins. He accepts him on the basis that he has placed 100 percent complete trust in Christ

Repentance is necessary for salvation, because it is a means of preparing the way for complete belief or trust to take place. Anything that conflicts with a person placing 100 percent trust in Christ for salvation must be repented of. Salvation repentance is to believe on Christ to the exclusion of every other object of belief or trust.

The baptismal regeneration crowd has as much Bible basis for *washing sins away* as some have for *turning from sins*. Their way really makes more sense because you can complete your part of salvation, get out of the baptistry, and dry off. You never can completely turn from your sins.

The Bible does not refer to Christians as *turners* but as *believers*. If your salvation is based on turning from your sins, you may doubt your salvation when you find sin in your life. You need to have faith in Christ, not faith in your own ability to turn from your sins.

# CONFLICTING SIGNS CONFUSE SINNERS

JESUS: SAVIOR OR SAVIOR'S ASSISTANT?

Dear Jesus,
   Let me help you save me, OK? I now turn from my sins and trust you. Thank you for saving me with my help. Amen.

JESUS: SAVIOR OR SEASONING?

Directions: Sprinkle a little bit of Jesus on your reformation. Season to taste. Note: Use as a substitute for complete trust in Christ. This substitute is very versatile and can be used in any situation where the unbeliever wants to play a role in their salvation.

JESUS: SAVIOR OR SUPPLEMENT?

If turning from your sins doesn't do the job alone, just add Jesus.

JESUS: SAVIOR OR BUILDING INSPECTOR?

Dear Jesus,
   I got rid of some of my sins to make room for you in my heart. Come in, take a look, and tell me what you think.

JESUS: SAVIOR OR MERCHANT?

Dear Jesus,
   I believe you died for me. Now will you please save me if I turn from my sins in return? Thank you.

> Jesus is not an assistant, a seasoning,
> a supplement, a building inspector,
> or even a merchant.

**REPENT OF YOUR SINS**

You'd better stop *trading* and start *trusting*.
You'd better stop *bargaining* and start *believing*.
You'd better stop *dealing* and start *depending*.

## WRONG ROUTE #2
# CONFESS YOUR SINS

Altar Worker: Now that you know that Jesus died for you, you need to confess your sins to be saved.

Child: Dear Jesus, please forgive me for the time I hit my little sister and for the time I lied to my mom. Forgive me for cheating on that test at school and for throwing a paper airplane in class. Forgive me for the time I stole a cookie and for the time I threw away my vegetables instead of eating them. Forgive me for the time I hit Charlie at the playground and for the time . . . and for playing in the mud when my dad told me not to and for not wearing my gloves and hat to school when it was cold outside. Please forgive me for pulling the hair off my sister's doll and for breaking Mom's favorite china plate. I hope I didn't forget anything Lord. Amen.

# CONFLICTING SIGNS CONFUSE SINNERS

OF COURSE THIS child's prayer is a bit exaggerated, but if we believe we need to confess our sins in order to get saved, then what should we do? What sins in particular are the most important ones to confess? Should we just confess the sins we can remember? Maybe we need to confess only recent sins. What if we only confess the really bad sins? If we are not Bible students, how are we going to know what's a sin and what's not? Are we still responsible for confessing the sins we are committing if we're unaware that they are in fact sins? These questions must be answered if we are to understand the role of confession of sins in salvation.

## Confession and Salvation

Confession of sins is the believer's route to forgiveness and cleansing, not the sinner's route to salvation. Many believers use 1 John 1:9 to make a case for sinners confessing their sins. It says, "If we confess our sins, he is faithful and just to forgive us our sins, and to cleanse us from all unrighteousness." Verses 3 and 4 of 1 John 1 give us a better idea of the intended audience. "That which we have seen and heard declare we unto you, that ye also may have fellowship with us: and truly our fellowship is with the Father, and with his Son Jesus Christ. And these things write we unto you, that your joy may be full." Clearly, 1 John was written to believers to show them how to maintain fellowship with the Father and how to have joy. It was not written to sinners to help lead them to Christ.

The sinner's route to salvation is found in John 3:16: "For God so loved the world, that he gave his only begotten Son, that whosoever believeth in him should not perish, but have everlasting life." In Acts 16:29-31 we read about the Philippian jailer. "Then he called for a light, and sprang in, and came trembling, and fell down before Paul and Silas, And brought them out, and said, Sirs, what must I do to be saved? And they said, Believe on the Lord Jesus Christ, and thou shalt be saved, and thy house." Neither of these passages makes any mention of confessing sins. The only requirement for salvation is that you believe on the Lord Jesus Christ.

Many preachers and soul-winners are guilty of combining these two ideas together in their gospel presentation. If a sinner thinks he has to confess sins to get saved, then he may think he has to confess sins, once saved, in order to remain saved. We must be careful to give a clear presentation of the gospel. Don't let your good intentions provide a basis for the new believer to later doubt his salvation or to think he can possibly lose it.

In order for a person to be saved, he must confess—admit or agree—with God that he is a sinner. But confessing that he is a sinner is not the same as confessing his sins.

## WRONG ROUTE #3
## GIVE UP YOUR BAD HABITS

IF YOU BELIEVE that you need to give up a bad habit to get saved, then each person's road to salvation will be different. If the roads are all different, then they cannot all be right. There is only one road to heaven, and that is through complete trust in Jesus Christ.

Many good, well-meaning preachers have changed a good motive into a false means of salvation. A person's bad habit may reveal the need for salvation, and the desire to have deliverance from it may be a good motive for seeking salvation. However, we should not change a motive to a means by stating or implying that Christ will save only in exchange for one's willingness to give up these sins. To trust Christ to save you in exchange for your willingness to give up some sins is false or misplaced trust. In this case the trust is in what you are not doing instead of what Christ did on the cross. This trade with God makes salvation something you obtain yourself rather than something you receive as a gift by placing your faith in Christ, which is also a gift. (see Eph. 2:8–9.)

The belief that you must give up a bad habit as a prerequisite to salvation probably hinders many people from getting saved. Does a person who has a problem with smoking have to give it up in order to go to heaven? What about an alcoholic? How about a person who gossips? What about someone who is a glutton? What makes one sin worse than another? Who said certain sins are acceptable? All sin is repulsive in God's sight. It often appears that those telling the sinner how to be saved will select certain sins—those they are not committing themselves—for the sinner to give up in order to be saved.

Does an individual need to be righteous in order to receive salvation? No, but if you ask a potential convert to give up gambling before he can get saved isn't that what you are implying? Romans 3:10 says, "As it is written, There is none righteous, no, not one." We see the same idea in Isaiah 64:6a, "But we are all as an unclean thing, and all our righteousnesses are as filthy rags." Clearly

GIVE UP YOUR BAD HABITS

no one is righteous because of his or her own deeds. We are righteous because of what Christ has done. "For as by one man's disobedience many were made sinners, so by the obedience of one shall many be made righteous" (Rom. 5:19). The Lord viewed Lot as righteous, even though none of his actions would seem to indicate it. "And delivered just Lot, vexed with the filthy conversation of the wicked: (For that righteous man dwelling among them, in seeing and hearing, vexed his righteous soul from day to day with their unlawful deeds)" (2 Pet. 2:7–8). Not only are we declared to be righteous, but we are also now called sons of God. In John 1:12 we read, "But as many as received him, to them gave he power to become the Sons of God, even to them that believe on his name."

> Can you place 99 percent of your faith in Jesus
> and give up a really bad sin to get saved?

If one of God's children can still have a problem with drinking or smoking, does it make sense to tell an unbeliever that he must give up these sins in order to receive salvation? In fact, before an individual is saved, all of his "righteousness" counts for nothing. We need to offer salvation to all who are willing to receive it and let the Holy Spirit help them clean up their lives after they are saved.

## The Rich Young Ruler

In Mark 10:17–22 Jesus dealt with a man who wanted to inherit eternal life. Jesus asked him to go sell what he had and give to the poor so that he would have treasures in heaven. Did Jesus ask the man to give up his wealth so he could get saved? What was the purpose behind his statement? Verse 23 says, "And Jesus looked round about, and saith unto his disciples, How hardly shall they that have riches enter into the kingdom of God!" Why? In verses 24 and 25 we see the answer. "And the disciples were astonished at his words. But Jesus answereth again, and saith unto them, Children, how hard is it for them that trust in riches to enter into the kingdom of God! It is easier for a camel to go through the eye of a needle, than for a rich man to enter into the kingdom of God."

If you trust in your riches, why would you trust in Jesus? In order for people to receive salvation they must see their need of it. Jesus said riches could get in the way of this man's salvation. In Jesus' day, as in our time, many falsely believed that having wealth was a sign from God of His approval on their lives. This false assurance keeps many wealthy people from taking time even to hear the plan of salvation much less to receive it.

### Interview with a "Believer"

Interviewer: Believer, what did you do to get Christ to save you?

"Believer": I gave up my sins and I said, "Come on in."

Interviewer: Do you mean to say that giving up your sins is your way of saying your trust is in Christ?

"Believer": Yeah, something like that.

Interviewer: It sounds to me like your trust is in giving up your sins and not in Christ.

"Believer": Yeah, well Psalm 66:18 says, "If I regard iniquity in my heart the Lord will not hear me," so I've got to get rid of my sins before He'll hear my prayer for salvation.

## CONFLICTING SIGNS CONFUSE SINNERS

Interviewer: You are not a believer; you are an unsaved sinner who thinks he's a believer. Giving up your sins to earn acceptance from Christ doesn't make you a believer. You are just going from unbelief to false belief. You must give up your false belief and trust in Christ to receive salvation.

## WRONG ROUTE #4
## BE CONVICTED OF YOUR SINS

A FAIRLY COMMON belief in many Christian circles is that people cannot get saved unless they are first convicted of their sins. Does this mean that they know they are sinners or does this mean they feel bad about their sins? How bad do they need to feel before they are ready to get saved? Would this be evidenced by tears or by the appearance that they are carrying around the weight of the world on their shoulders? Could sufficient conviction occur during an evangelistic service, or must an individual be convicted for a period of days or weeks before they can get saved?

Feeling conviction for one's sins can be a good motive for getting saved but let's not turn it into a requirement. One definition that Webster gives for conviction is "the act of convincing a person of error or of compelling the admission of truth."[1] When most people use the word *convicted* I believe they mean that someone feels really bad about their sin. The only conviction that is really necessary is to know that you are a sinner in need of a Savior. It doesn't matter how bad you feel about your sin; if you don't trust Christ you cannot receive salvation.

## Conviction Yes, Salvation No

The only reference to conviction in the King James translation is in John 8:9: "And they which heard it, being convicted by their own conscience, went out one by one, beginning at the eldest, even unto the last: and Jesus was left alone, and the woman standing in the midst." Who were these people? They were the scribes and Pharisees who brought to Jesus a woman caught in adultery. Were they convicted of their sins? Yes. Did they get saved? No. They all walked away because they were unwilling to trust in Jesus for salvation. They came in feeling self-righteous and left feeling convicted of their own sin. Without salvation the conviction of their own sin didn't do any good.

In John 16:8 we read, "And when he is come, he will reprove the world of sin, and of righteousness, and of judgment:" In this verse the unsaved—or the world—is reproved of sin. The word *reprove* means to bring to light, to expose, to convict and convince. The Holy Spirit convicts the world of one particular sin, the sin of unbelief. John 16:9a continues: "Of sin, because they believe not on me." It is unbelief that condemns the lost sinner, not his committing individual sins. We know this because in John 3:18 Jesus said, "He that believeth on him is not condemned: but he that believeth not is condemned already, because he hath not believed in the name of the only begotten Son of God."

This discussion of conviction raises some interesting questions that need to be addressed:

# BE CONVICTED OF YOUR SINS

WHAT IF I FEEL CONVICTED OF DRINKING ALCOHOL AND I PROMISE GOD THAT I WILL STOP DRINKING IF HE WILL SAVE ME? WILL I GET SAVED?

The problem with this scenario is that it is backwards. Trust Jesus to save you first. Then ask Him to help you with your alcohol problem.

WHAT WOULD A LITTLE CHILD FEEL CONVICTED OF?

If the focus is on conviction, you might prevent children from getting saved. Teach children that they are sinners in need of a Savior. Don't worry about whether or not they feel convicted.

IF I DON'T FEEL CONVICTED CAN I STILL GET SAVED?

Absolutely. All you need is to know you are a sinner. Trust in Jesus completely to save you.

IF CONVICTION IS USED TO BRING PEOPLE TO SALVATION, WHAT DO THEY DO WHEN THEY SIN AND FEEL CONVICTED AFTER THEY GET SAVED? DO THEY GET SAVED AGAIN?

No. What they really need to learn is how to get rid of a problem with sin. First John 1:9 describes it clearly: "If we confess our sins, he is faithful and just to forgive us our sins, and to cleanse us from all unrighteousness." Confessing your sin will bring forgiveness and cleansing. To help overcome a particular sin, learn what God's Word says about it. Then memorize specific verses you can use when temptation arises.

# WRONG ROUTE #5
# SORROW FOR YOUR SINS

IN 2 CORINTHIANS 7:10 WE read, "For godly sorrow worketh repentance to salvation not to be repented of: but the sorrow of the world worketh death." This verse is the primary basis of the teaching on sorrowing for sins in order to receive salvation.

Should you be sorry for your sins? Is telling God that you are sorry for your sins an apology? When must you be sorry for your sins? These questions will be addressed in this chapter.

Let's start with some synonyms:

> apologetic—showing regret[1]
> apologize—confessing oneself to be at fault[2]

If a person does not show or express sorrow for their sins, they are sometimes called unrepentant. This line of reasoning is based on the premise that the Scriptures command the sinner to "repent of his sin." However, a careful study of Scripture will reveal that the Bible doesn't make that statement. The Scripture actually says something entirely different: "Repent ye, and believe the gospel" (Mark 1:15b). One of the definitions of *repent* means to *change your mind.* When a person hears the gospel of Christ and completely trusts Christ to save him to the exclusion of all other beliefs, that is a change of mind. He has repented.

So what is the godly sorrow mentioned in 2 Corinthians 7:10? Let's take a closer look at this scripture. Does it actually teach that a lost soul must sorrow over his sin in order to receive eternal life? The apostle Paul is writing again to the church at Corinth. The church at Corinth, as with every New Testament church, was made up of saved, baptized believers. This group of believers had sinned and erred greatly in not rebuking open sin in the church, where a man had taken his father's wife (1 Corinthians 5:1-13). The church did not rebuke the son nor come to the rescue of the father. They were in danger of losing their testimony in the community, their effectiveness for God, and their power with God. Paul was sorry that he had to rebuke them, which in turn made them sorrowful. When the church obeyed Paul and put the fornicator out of their fellowship, they were saved. Second Corinthians 7:11 describes their salvation. Their testimony in the community was saved. Their fellowship with Paul went unbroken and was saved.

It should be clear to the reader that the salvation spoken of in 2 Corinthians 7:10 is not the eternal salvation of the individual soul from hell to heaven. It is rather the salvation of a body of believers and a local church from lost fellowship, lost power, and a lost testimony in the community.

## Soul Winning and Sorrow

What purpose does it serve for the soul-winner, to determine if the sinner is sorry for her sins after she gives her the plan of salvation, but before she invites her to trust Christ as Savior? Does being sorry for or expressing sadness or grief over your sins make Christ more willing to forgive? Does it make the sinner more qualified to receive forgiveness? If not, then what is the purpose of having the salvation prospect express sorrow for her sins?

Jesus died for all of our sins: "Who his own self bare our sins in his own body on the tree, that we, being dead to sins, should live unto righteousness: by whose stripes ye were healed" (1 Peter 2:24). He died not only for our past sins but also for our future sins. When the sinner trusts Christ as Savior, he instantly receives forgiveness from the penalty of all of his sins, past, present, and future. "He that believeth on the Son hath everlasting life: and he that believeth not the Son shall not see life, but the wrath of God abideth on him" (John 3:36). If the sinner hears he must be sorry for his sins before God will save him from the penalty of them, then he would have to be sorry for his future sins before he got saved and before he committed them. Does it make sense that a person should be made to sorrow over past sins as a prerequisite to salvation from the penalty of past, present, and future sins?

If you sorrow over specific sins, you must identify them. (see Rom. 7:7.) If you identify sins, this would necessitate a thorough Bible study. If it is only necessary to sorrow over the sins that each is aware of, then the more Bible a person knows, the more sins they'd have to sorrow over. This person would have more obstacles preventing their salvation than the person who knows nothing about the Bible.

At best, being troubled over or sorrowing over one's sins might be a good motive to get saved. Unfortunately, it serves no purpose and rather becomes an obstacle when the preacher or soul-winner brings it up and insists that God will withhold salvation from the sinner until he is sorry for some of them. A good motive for wanting to be saved then becomes a false means of obtaining salvation or at best is an unnecessary obstacle. Jesus died for ALL sinners, sorrowing or not, and he'll save any sinner who trusts Him, sorrowing or not.

What scriptural basis does someone have who teaches that sorrow for sins must precede salvation? We have seen numerous Bible tracts that quote 2 Corinthians 7:10 and then say something like this: "If you are sorry for your sins then pray this prayer and ask Christ to save you."

There is nothing wrong with a sinner's feeling or expressing sorrow for his sins while he is trusting Christ to save him. It is wrong, however, for someone to tell a sinner he must be sorry for his sins in order to receive salvation.

> Can you talk Jesus into saving you
> by being sorry for your sins?

Here's the picture. A sinner first needs to be saved from hell, the penalty that all sinners owe. The sinner is a sinner by his birth. "Wherefore, as by one man [Adam] sin entered into the world, and death by sin; and so death passed upon all men, for that all have sinned" (Rom. 5:12). If he had to be sorry for the reason he was going to hell, he would have to be sorry he was born. If he must sorrow for someone's sins in order to be saved, then let him be sorry for Adam's sin. "For as by one man's disobedience [Adam] many were made sinners, so by the obedience of one [Jesus] shall many be made righteous" (Rom. 5:19).

## Do You Limit Soul-winning?

The belief in sorrow for sins limits soul-winning to the church service. Pastors whose people don't win souls and who themselves only win souls in the church on Sunday morning are often seeking only for sorrowing sinners. The unsaved man who is willing to come to the church service is more likely to be sorrowing for some sins, or more likely to be made to sorrow by something he hears preached. The average John Doe sinner who is not thinking about church or God or his sins is not a candidate for salvation based on this belief. The belief that a sinner must sorrow for his sins before God will save him is neither a friend to the plan of salvation nor to biblical door-to-door, one-on-one soul-winning.

## Sorrow for Sin in the Life of a Believer

Sorrow for sins along with identifying, confessing, and repenting of an individual's sins all belong to the child of God and are part of his or her relationship with the Heavenly Father. However, when sorrow for sins is used as a prerequisite to salvation, it becomes an obstacle and prevents salvations from taking place. These beliefs also prevent Christians from becoming soul-winners and witnessing one-on-one. Let's keep the plan of salvation clear!

# WRONG ROUTE #6
# GIVE YOUR HEART TO JESUS

HAVE YOU EVER heard anyone tell someone to give his or her heart to Jesus? This sounds good, but what does it really mean? One of the references to salvation and the heart is found in Romans 10:9–10: "That if thou shalt confess with thy mouth the Lord Jesus, and shalt believe in thine *heart* that God hath raised him from the dead, thou shalt be saved. For with the *heart* man believeth unto righteousness; and with the mouth confession is made unto salvation" (author's emphasis). To help us understand what this means, let's start by contrasting head belief with heart belief.

## Head Belief vs. Heart Belief

Some seem to teach that when people believe from the head, they acknowledge the biblical fact of Christ's death and resurrection. If they add sorrowing, confessing, and repenting of sins, then they are believing with the heart. The real difference in believing with the heart instead of the head does not involve an emotional component; it is the object of belief that's different. It is not how one believes but what or whom a person believes. When we believe from the heart instead of the head, we're not sorrowing for our sins, repenting of our sin, confessing our sins, or being convicted of our sins. Believing with the heart is not a different kind of belief; it is a more complete belief.

Philip wouldn't baptize the Ethiopian eunuch until he believed with all his heart. "And as they went on their way, they came unto a certain water: and the eunuch said, See, here is water, what doth hinder me to be baptized? And Philip said, If thou believest with all thine heart, thou mayest. And he answered and said, I believe that Jesus Christ is the Son of God" (Acts 8:36–37). Philip made it clear that the eunuch could only be saved if he was completely trusting in Christ. After one believes (acknowledges) Jesus died on the cross to save sinners, he or she believes on Him (places all faith in Him, completely trusts Him) to save him or her.

> Did you ask Jesus to come into your heart after you got rid of all your sins to make room for Him?

## Half-hearted Belief

Another way to describe what it means to believe with your heart is to compare whole-hearted belief with half-hearted belief. Half-hearted belief is incomplete trust in Christ, while believing with the heart represents whole-hearted or complete trust in Christ. If you are only half-heartedly believing in Jesus for salvation and partially trusting in something else for salvation, you are not really trusting in Jesus at all. You might be trying to turn from your sins or to give up a bad habit. Only Jesus can help you clean up your life. Trust in Him with your whole heart.

When you are leading an individual to Christ and you tell Him to believe with your heart, you have explained repentance. Salvation repentance is to believe on Christ to the exclusion of every other object of belief or trust. If a prospect with whom I shared the gospel trusted Christ then picked up his beer and finished it, I wouldn't doubt the sincerity of his repentance. He could have believed with his whole heart. But if that same individual started counting beads on a rosary, I would wonder if he had only half-heartedly believed on Christ. Make sure when you are soul-winning that you explain what it means to believe with your whole heart. Don't accept anything less than complete trust.

In the Bible there is no promise of everlasting life to those who partially believe in Christ. Christ is not an additive or a supplement. If you want to be saved, you must completely trust in Him.

Let's teach sinners to completely trust Christ to save them from the penalty of sin. Then, once saved, they can trust Christ to save them more completely from the power and practice of sin.

## WRONG ROUTE #7
## LIVE IT OR LOSE IT

DO YOU STOP SINNING TO GET SAVED?
DO YOU STOP SINNING TO STAY SAVED?

Holy Joe:   Knock, knock.

St. Peter:   Who's there?

Holy Joe:   It's me, Holy Joe, you know, the guy who used to be an alcoholic and a drug addict. I got saved, I cleaned up my life, and I never went back to my old sinful ways.

# CONFLICTING SIGNS CONFUSE SINNERS

St. Peter: What do you want?

Holy Joe: I want in! This is heaven, isn't it?

St Peter: Well, yes.

Holy Joe: So what's the problem?

St. Peter: Let me check the Book of Life.

Holy Joe: Why? Doesn't my record speak for itself?

St. Peter: No. The only way you can enter heaven is if you trusted in Jesus completely for your salvation.

Holy Joe: Well OK. Make sure you look under H for holy.

St. Peter: Well Joe, here's your name right here. Its under S for Smith. Joe Smith.

You may enter.

...Two hours later...

Holy Joe: St. Peter, there must be some mistake.

St. Peter: What's the problem.

Holy Joe: It's my neighbor, Unholy John. He was a drunk until the day he died.

St. Peter: What's your point?

Holy Joe: I must be in the wrong heaven or you put me in the wrong neighborhood or something.

St. Peter: Listen Joe. Do you remember how your name wasn't under H. Well John's name wasn't under U. You are here only by the grace of God. If you're not happy here, well, there's only one other option.

# LIVE IT OR LOSE IT

HOLY JOE REFORMED his life from drugs and alcohol and didn't commit any other "major" sins. He assumed he was saved because Christ approved of his lifestyle. The real reason he was saved was because he put his complete trust in Christ for salvation. Since Joe believed he was keeping himself saved by living a holy life, this effected how he saw both himself and others.

## Can You Lose Your Salvation by Sinning?

The concept of *live it or lose it* implies that you can lose your salvation by sinning. Suppose that after church on Sunday I'm driving my car at sixty mph in a fifty-five mph zone. Clearly I'm sinning, but will it cause me to lose my salvation? Most people would say no. What if I commit adultery? Would that cause me to lose my salvation? Many would say yes.

What's the difference between these two sins? I think everyone would agree that committing adultery is far more serious than going five miles over the speed limit. Does God judge us in this way? Would He accept the speeder into his presence but not the adulterer?

God is perfectly holy. It only took one "small" sin to separate Adam and Eve from God's presence. Eating from the tree of the knowledge of good and evil separated Adam and Eve from God. It required a sacrifice to remedy this. The idea that big sins but not small ones put our salvation in jeopardy is false. The only reason we can have salvation is because Jesus died on the cross for our sins. The only way we can receive salvation is by faith.

## Salvation by Faith

The Bible clearly states that we are not justified by the works of the law. All who are trying to make it to heaven because they don't commit any "big" sins are in trouble. Galatians 2:16 states, "Knowing that a man is not justified by the works of the law, but by the faith of Jesus Christ, even we have believed in Jesus Christ, that we might be justified by the faith of Christ, and not by the works of the law: for by the works of the law shall no flesh be justified." That verse says it pretty clearly. Two more verses in Galatians also emphasize faith, not works:

> I do not frustrate the grace of God: for if righteousness come by the law, then Christ is dead in vain.
> (Gal. 2:21)

> But that no man is justified by the law in the sight of God, it is evident: for, The just shall live by faith.
> (Gal. 3:11)

Not only do these verses state that we are saved by faith, but also that we are not saved by the law (living right). In addition Titus 3:5a says, "Not by works of righteousness which we have done, but according to his mercy he saved us." In Romans 3:28 we read, "Therefore, we conclude that a man is justified by faith without the deeds of the law." Let's not forget about Ephesians 2:8–9. "For by grace are ye saved through faith; and that not of yourselves: it is the gift of God: Not of works, lest any man should boast." Clearly we are saved by faith in Jesus Christ and not by our own works.

Can you promise Jesus you'll live right<br>in return for salvation?

## No Sin in Heaven

I (Paul) have heard the comment made that there is no sin in heaven. The implication is if you don't get rid of all the sin in your life, you won't be able to go to heaven. In 1 John 1:10 we read, "If we say that we have not sinned, we make him a liar, and his word is not in us." No believer is without sin.

If every believer sins, then why is there no sin in heaven? While believers are here on earth we have two natures. The Apostle Paul knew that there was a battle going on inside of him between these two natures. "For I know that in me (that is, in my flesh.) dwelleth no good thing: for to will is present with me; but how to perform that which is good I find not. For the good that I would I do not: but the evil which I would not, that I do" (Rom. 7:18–19). If the Apostle Paul had a battle between his natures, how can we expect to live without sin?

When we die and go to heaven, we will not live in our earthly bodies but in our glorified ones. "Behold, I show you a mystery; We shall not all sleep, but we shall all be changed, In a moment, in the twinkling of a eye, at the last trump: for the trumpet shall sound, and the dead shall be raised incorruptible, and we shall be changed. For this corruptible must put on incorruption, and this mortal must put on immortality" (1 Cor. 15:51–53). Our flesh will be done away with and replaced with an immortal body that will live forever with God in heaven. We will no longer have a sin nature.

While we are on earth, we need to remember that Jesus' death on the cross paid the price for our sins. We will never be able to live sin-free lives while we are here on earth.

## Chastisement of the Believer

Many Christians think that it is somehow unfair for God to allow Christians to continue sinning. Isn't there any penalty for a Christian who lives in sin, they ask? Yes,

## CONFLICTING SIGNS CONFUSE SINNERS

there certainly is, but it involves God's chastisement of the believer, not the loss of salvation.

> Heaven is your gift when you believe in Christ;
> Then out of love you dedicate your life.
> If you serve your Savior from a motive of love,
> your rewards will be great at the judgment above.

In 1 Corinthians 11:27–32 we read about how God chastises believers:

> Wherefore whosoever shall eat this bread, and drink this cup of the Lord, unworthily, shall be guilty of the body and blood of the Lord. But let a man examine himself, and so let him eat of that bread, and drink of that cup. For he that eateth and drinketh unworthily, eateth and drinketh damnation to himself, not discerning the Lord's body. For this cause many are weak and sickly among you, and many sleep. For if we would judge ourselves, we should not be judged. But when we are judged, we are chastened of the Lord, that we should not be condemned with the world.

This passage was written to believers about remembering the Lord's death. Before taking the Lord's Supper, we are to examine ourselves for the presence of sin. If we do this, we will not be judged. However, failure to do this brings judgment upon ourselves. This does not involve loss of eternal salvation but rather chastisement in the form of illness and death (v. 30). Both of these consequences involve our physical bodies, not our souls.

When believers fail to confess their sins, there are not only earthly penalties for sin but eternal penalties as well. In 1 Corinthians 3:13–15 we read:

> Every man's work shall be made manifest: for the day shall declare it, because it shall be revealed by fire; and the fire shall try every man's work of what sort it is. If any man's work abide which he hath built thereupon, he shall receive a reward. If any man's work shall be burned, he shall suffer loss: but he himself shall be saved; yet so as by fire.

Apparently there will be some people in heaven who did not live for God nor work for Him with proper motives. These individuals will suffer loss of rewards.

We will also have to give account for our words. "But I say unto you, That every idle word that men shall speak, they shall give account thereof in the day of judgment. For by thy words thou shalt be justified. and by thy words thou shalt be condemned" (Matt. 12:36–37). Some of us will have much to give account for!

Some Christians live their lives under the judgment of the chastening hand of their Heavenly Father. This is because they fail to judge themselves by not considering the consequences of the sin they're about to commit or because they don't confess their sin after they commit it. These Christians are not likely to earn many or any rewards in heaven. On the other hand, the Christian who out of fear of losing his salvation keeps his life clean and serves the Lord may see his works deemed unacceptable because of his improper motive.

## Jesus Paid it All

The problem with those who believe one can lose one's salvation is a fundamental misunderstanding of what Christ did. They feel somehow responsible for their salvation. These individuals want to do something to deserve it, so they try to keep their lives free from sin so they feel more

## CONFLICTING SIGNS CONFUSE SINNERS

deserving. They also tell themselves that if they fall into sin they will lose their salvation.

> If you can lose your salvation by sinning,
> then it means you have a conditional salvation.
> Jesus will save you,
> as long as you stay out of sin.
> Did Jesus save you or did He put you on probation?

Jesus paid the penalty for our sin. All of it. We don't pay anything and we can't do anything to deserve it. If you think that you need to pay part of the price, you are no different that the heathens. Practitioners of every other religion are also trying to work their way to heaven.

It's not easy to believe only on Christ. It's easier to believe on Christ plus something else. Which is easier, jumping from a burning building into the firemen's net or climbing down the fire escape? Most people would rather trust their own climbing ability than to put their faith in the firemen.

A comparison of future judgments for believers and unbelievers, may help you better understand what will happen to believers who lead sinful lives. Their sinful lives will adversely affect the quality of their service for the Lord and will shorten their lifespan, which will limit the quantity of their service.

### FUTURE JUDGMENTS

| Believers (saved) Judgment | Unbelievers (unsaved) Judgment |
|---|---|
| The Judgment Seat of Christ  Judgment for service  to determine rewards | The White Throne Judgment  Judgment for sin to determine retribution |

## LIVE IT OR LOSE IT

| | |
|---|---|
| No one goes to hell. | No one goes to heaven. |
| Only believers are present. | Unsaved are present for judgment; saved are present to condemn. (Matt. 12:41) |
| Includes all believers, both dead and living (1 Thes. 4:17, 2 Tim. 4:1) | |
| Believers' judgment for sin is past No condemnation for those in Christ (Rom. 8:1) | |

If it appears difficult to keep your salvation, don't you suppose some unbelievers decide they wouldn't be able to keep it so they ask themselves, "Why bother to get saved?"

When we trust Christ as our Savior, we receive forgiveness from the penalty of all our sins. The moment God sees our faith in Christ, our judgment as sinners has forever past. We call this judicial forgiveness. From that moment forward, our sins as God's children are forgiven when we confess them to our loving Heavenly Father. Failure to confess our sins as children of God may result in chastisement. "For if we would judge ourselves, we should not be judged. But when we are judged, we are chastened of the Lord, that we should not be condemned with the world" (2 Cor. 11:31–32).

So *live it* (a life of unbroken fellowship), or *lose it* (salvation from the penalty of sin), are not even the same. How we live the first *it*, has no effect on the second *it*, neither positive nor negative.

## WRONG ROUTE #8
. . . . . . . . . . . . . . . . . . . . . . . . . . . . . . . . . .
# KEEP THE FAITH

Did you get saved when you trusted Jesus to save you, or is it a process that continues until you die or quit following?

# CONFLICTING SIGNS CONFUSE SINNERS

## The Birthday Present

Father: Son, come out to the garage. I want to show you something. For your eighteenth birthday your mother and I bought a gift for you.

Son: Wow, a new car! Thanks dad. Now I won't ever have to wait for a ride again. Can I drive it around the block a couple of times?

Father: Son, before you try it out, there are a few things I need to explain to you.

First of all, your mother and I didn't completely pay for the car. We only made a down payment on it. So now you're responsible to keep up the payments of $268.59 every month. In addition, you'll have to pay for the car tax, the new tags, and of course the insurance.

Son: But dad, that sounds like a lot of money! How will I ever pay for it?

Father: Well son, now that you have your own transportation, you should be able to get a job.

Son: Well can I at least take a short ride to try it out before I go job hunting?

Father: We didn't talk about the maintenance schedule yet.

Son: What maintenance schedule?

Father: Every Saturday you're expected to wash, wax, and vacuum the car. Every 3,000 miles you need to change the oil and oil filter and rotate the tires.

Son: What happens if I miss a payment or the oil doesn't get changed when it should?

# KEEP THE FAITH

Father: Son, you're allowed only three minor violations of this agreement. If you have a major violation, like missing a car payment, then your mother and I will have to take the car away from you.

HAVE YOU EVER heard the salvation message explained in a manner like this? In order to get saved, you need to believe in Jesus to save you from the penalty of sin. That's the start of your salvation. Then you must continue to believe in Him as demonstrated by attending church, reading your Bible, etc., if you want to go to heaven. To stop doing these things would show that you no longer believe and would result in the loss your salvation. It sounds like God made the down payment on your salvation but you must keep up the payments by maintaining a Christian lifestyle. Did God give you a gift or sell you a car?

*Do we make heaven seem like an impossible destination by adding requirements to get there?*

The idea that Christians must demonstrate their belief by maintaining a Christian lifestyle comes from verses such as Titus 3:8a: "This is a faithful saying, and these things I will that thou affirm constantly, that they which have believed in God might be careful to maintain good works." The apostle Paul also seems to be promoting this idea in 2 Timothy 4:7, where he says, "I have fought a good fight, I have finished my course, I have kept the faith." These verses seem to imply that a person needs to follow Christ if he expects to remain in Christ. The implication is that if you don't continue to follow Christ or keep the faith, you will lose your salvation.

## CONFLICTING SIGNS CONFUSE SINNERS

When you believe on Jesus Christ for salvation from the penalty of sin, you are saved. This puts you "in Christ" (2 Cor. 5:17). You're going to heaven because you're in Christ.

> If you can lose your salvation
> by not following Jesus,
> then it means you have a conditional salvation.
> Jesus will save you
> as long as you follow Him.

The teachings of Jesus are also used to support the idea that you follow Jesus to remain in Him. Matthew 7:13–14 says, "Enter ye in at the strait gate: for wide is the gate, and broad is the way, that leadeth to destruction, and many there be which go in thereat; Because strait is the gate, and narrow is the way, which leadeth unto life, and few there be that find it." This verse seems to imply that many people believe on Christ, at least initially, but later fall away for various reasons, and only a few people stick with it in order to get to heaven. Luke 13:23–24 says, "Then said one unto him, Lord, are there few that be saved? And he said unto them, Strive to enter in at the strait gate: for many, I say unto you, will seek to enter in, and shall not be able." Jesus makes it sound as though salvation is a rather difficult process. In order to understand these passages you must make a distinction between salvation and discipleship.

## Salvation vs. Discipleship

Is it really difficult to obtain salvation? In John 3:16 we read, "For God so loved the world, that he gave his only begotten Son, that whosoever believeth in him should not perish, but have everlasting life." How are we saved? By believing. The moment you believe on Jesus you are saved.

What are individuals doing when they keep the faith, stick to the narrow way, or finish their course? They are disciples, because those who hold to Jesus' teachings are Jesus' disciples. Is every saved person a disciple? No. I know many Christians who don't hold to scriptural principles for their finances or marriage. Many are unwilling to fulfill their role in the body of Christ and some seldom attend church. Does this cause them to lose their salvation because they don't completely follow Christ? Paul gives us an answer in 1 Corinthians 3:10–15:

> According to the grace of God which is given unto me, as a wise master builder, I have laid the foundation, and another buildeth thereon. But let every man take heed how he buildeth thereupon. For other foundation can no man lay than that is laid, which is Jesus Christ. Now if any man build upon this foundation gold, silver, precious stones, wood, hay, stubble; Every man's work shall be made manifest: for the day shall declare it, because it shall be revealed by fire; and the fire shall try every man's work of what sort it is. If any man's work abide which he hath built thereupon, he shall receive a reward. If any man's work shall be burned, he shall suffer loss: but he himself shall be saved; yet so as by fire.

A good disciple builds using gold, silver, and costly stones, while a poor disciple builds using wood, hay, and straw. If you don't follow Christ you will lose your reward, but not your salvation.

## The Narrow Gate

Now let's deal with the small gate and the narrow way. The *gate* represents salvation, while the *way* represents the abundant life. Why is the gate small? It's because Jesus said:

## CONFLICTING SIGNS CONFUSE SINNERS

"Neither is there salvation in any other: for there is none other name under heaven given among men, whereby we must be saved" (Acts 4:12). There is only one way to enter through the gate that leads to life, which is by complete trust in Christ for salvation. The gate to hell is wide because you can enter believing many different things. You can believe in a false religion or a false cult leader. You can even go through the broad gate while you try to turn from your sins, confess your sins, sorrow for your sins, or give up a bad habit.

> Are we saved based on our belief in Jesus
> or based on our promise to follow Him?

Why is the *way* narrow? It's difficult to follow God's principles for finances. You must tithe, budget, and save. On the broad road you can spend your money any way you want. You can even max out your credit cards by spending money you don't have. Many Christians are on the broad road for their finances. How many do you know who stick to the narrow way? The same principle would apply to our tongues. On the narrow way you must give thanks in everything, build others up spiritually, and avoid gossip. On the broad way you can say whatever you like, anytime you want. These are just two examples that show why the way to life is narrow and difficult to stay on.

So did Jesus make the down payment on our salvation and leave us responsible for the balance? Not a chance! We could never keep our end of the bargain. Second Timothy 2:13 says, "If we believe not, yet he abideth faithful: he cannot deny himself." If we stop believing and start believing in other things, the Holy Spirit is still inside of us, and Jesus cannot deny us, even if we don't stick to the narrow way.

## KEEP THE FAITH

"For I know whom I have believed, and am persuaded that he is able to keep that which I have committed unto him against that day" (2 Tim. 1:12b).

## WRONG ROUTE #9
. . . . . . . . . . . . . . . . . . . . . . . . . . . .
# MAKE A PUBLIC PROFESSION OF FAITH

### The Aisle or Denial?

**W**HILE IT IS important to confess Christ publicly, the question is: Is it necessary for salvation? In Matthew 10:32–33 we read, "Whosoever therefore shall confess me before men, him will I confess also before my Father which is in heaven. But whosoever shall deny me before men, him will I also deny before my Father which is in heaven." Does this mean we will hear those words found in Matthew 7:23, "And then will I profess unto them, I never knew you; depart from me, ye that work iniquity." Let's read further. Matthew 10:37 says, "He that loveth father or mother more than me is not worthy of me: and he that loveth son or daughter more than me is not worthy of me. And he that taketh not his cross, and followeth after me, is not worthy of me. He that findeth his life shall lose it: and he that loseth his life for my sake shall find it." What does it mean when Jesus says he will deny us, or that that we are unworthy? Many would say that clearly this means that a person is not saved.

We have two examples in the New Testament of secret disciples. Joseph, of Arimathaea went from being a secret disciple to openly taking down the body of Jesus. "And after this Joseph, of Arimathaea, being a disciple of Jesus, but secretly for fear of the Jews, besought Pilate that he might take away the body of Jesus: and Pilate gave him leave. He came therefore, and took the body of Jesus" (John 19:38). We have a second example recorded in John 12:42: "Nevertheless among the chief rulers also many believed on him; but because of the Pharisees they did not confess him, lest they should be put out of the synagogue:" Clearly some believers in Jesus would not confess him openly because of the consequences of doing so.

Confessing Christ publicly can have different consequences depending on where you live. It is easy to confess Christ when you are around other believers, but what if you were asked to renounce your faith or be executed? Would a person not be saved or lose their salvation because they were unwilling to die for Christ?

Let's ask the question in reverse. Can you be saved only if you are willing to die for Jesus? It is important to remember that God will reward us for our deeds. "Who will render to every man according to his deeds" (Rom. 2:6). In Revelation 2:10 we read, "Fear none of those things which thou shalt suffer: behold, the devil shall cast some of you into prison, that ye may be tried; and ye shall have tribulation ten days: be thou faithful unto death, and I will give thee a crown of life." The reward here for dying for Jesus is a crown of life. Revelation 20:4 gives us another instance where Christians died for their faith:

> And I saw thrones, and they sat upon them, and judgment was given unto them: and I saw the souls of them that were beheaded for the witness of Jesus, and for the word of God, and which had not worshiped the beast, neither his image, neither had received his mark upon their foreheads, or in their hands; and they lived and reigned with Christ a thousand years.

The people mentioned in this verse died for their belief, and they will be able to reign with Christ.

Making a public profession of faith is very important. In the United States we are unlikely to suffer any serious consequences for doing so, but if you live in Saudi Arabia or China, it could cost you your life.

## The Aisle of Trepidation

Fear of walking an aisle keeps some people from getting saved. It may be the only time they have the opportunity to trust Christ. For example, as a child and teenager the only opportunity to get saved this author (Trent) had was during a church service. I knew at several times I needed and wanted to be saved but didn't want to go forward by myself in front of a crowd. I was afraid to go forward in front of other people. I remained unsaved until age twenty when someone told me how to be saved, and I eagerly accepted it. The fear barrier was not present in this situation. It was the first time anyone witnessed to me one on one.

We should also consider a person who trusts Christ as Savior at a time and place where a public profession may not be practical or advisable, such as at 2:00 A.M. in bed while watching a Christian television program. Would this person not be saved until he was able to get to the next available church service?

Encouraging the unsaved to walk an aisle can be helpful in many cases, but let's not make it a barrier to salvation by making it a requirement.

# WRONG ROUTE #10
## PRAY THROUGH

### Time-Consuming Salvations

11:59 A.M.
Pastor: If you want to be saved this morning, make your way down to the altar. No simple repeat-after-me prayer will do. I want you to kneel and pray from your heart. I want you to pray until you feel it. Pray until you know you've broken through. Pray until you know you have it. Pray until you know you're saved.

1:00 P.M.
Janitor: Did you get it?
Sinner: Not yet.

3:00 P.M.
Janitor: Did you get through?
Sinner: No, not yet.

## CONFLICTING SIGNS CONFUSE SINNERS

4:00 P.M.
Janitor: Wouldn't you like some lunch?
Sinner: No thanks. I haven't gotten through.

5:30 P.M.
Janitor: Are you sure you wouldn't like something to eat?
Sinner: No, I can't feel anything. I need to keep praying.

6:45 P.M.
Pastor: It's almost time for the evening service. Surely you must be finished.
Sinner: No, I really want to know I've touched God.
Pastor: Would you like to go to a Sunday school room to continue?
Sinner: Yes, that would be nice.

8:20 P.M.
Pastor: We're finished; how about you?
Sinner: No, I'm not there yet.

10:00 P.M.
Pastor: Oh, she's asleep. I guess she got it.

PRAYING THROUGH IS an idea that is not promoted much anymore. However, it is worth mentioning. The idea is that you can't just get saved. Rather, you must continue praying until you've broken through or until you know it's accomplished. Instead of confessing your sins or promising Jesus that you'll live for Him, the implication is that a certain amount of praying is required. You will know you have accomplished this by a feeling that you have.

The implication is that God's heart is hard, and much begging, pleading, and perhaps tears are necessary to soften God's heart and make Him more willing to save. The truth is that God is more willing to save than most sinners are willing to receive. Also remember that God is the one extending the offer to save. Praying or asking even one time is not even necessary. Just accept the offer.

The problem with the praying through approach is that it looks for a feeling. Trust God's Word by faith and feelings will follow.

## Begging God

Even though the idea of praying through may not be widely taught these days, many people still resort to this in an effort to get saved.

A relative of mine (Trent) came home from a church service and decided he needed to get saved. He prayed fervently for a couple of hours in agony begging God to save him. He was waiting for a feeling. He made a final statement to Jesus, "You said if I would believe on you, you would save me." He says he was immediately saved. What was the problem? Begging and pleading with God isn't a way to get saved. Tell Christ you are fully trusting in Him for salvation. For my relative, it appears that he didn't express trust in Christ's willingness to save him until the last statement he made.

# WRONG ROUTE #11
# MAKE JESUS LORD OF YOUR LIFE

> **PAY TOLL AHEAD**
> Give Your Life to Jesus!

### The Contract

The following dialogue takes place at the entrance to the sheepfold:

Lost Sheep: May I come in?

Gate Sheep: Did you sign a contract?

Lost Sheep: What contract?

# CONFLICTING SIGNS CONFUSE SINNERS

Gate Sheep: You know, the contract that every sheep signs in order to enter the fold.

Lost Sheep: What's in the contract?

Gate Sheep: It's an agreement between you and the shepherd. Here's a copy for you to read.

I _____ (sheepfold applicant) do hereby agree to the following conditions as a prerequisite for entering the sheepfold:

1. I agree to arise at 5:00 A.M. every morning to go to the pasture.
2. I agree to abide by all sheepfold rules.
3. I agree to read my wool production manual three times per week.
4. I agree to give 10 percent of my wool to the general fold fund.
5. I agree to give of my time to the upkeep of the pasture fence.
6. I agree to faithfully attend all sheepfold meetings.
7. I agree to make myself available to fill a fold office should the need arise.

The undersigned applicant does hereby agree to abide by all sheepfold conditions to the best of his ability and will not knowingly violate any of the rules, policies, or procedures of the sheepfold commission.

_____   _____
(sheepfold applicant)           (date)

_____   _____
(sheepfold entrance manager)    (date)

## The Two Lords

MANY PEOPLE BELIEVE that the only way you can be saved is to make Jesus the Lord of your life. Verses such as Romans 10:9 are used to support this argument. "That if thou shalt confess with thy mouth the Lord Jesus, and shalt believe in thine heart that God hath raised him from the dead, thou shalt be saved." Since it doesn't say Jesus Christ it says the Lord Jesus some would say this must mean you have to make him totally Lord.

Let's look at another passage where the term Lord is used. "That at the name of Jesus every knee should bow, of things in heaven, and things in earth, and things under the earth; And that every tongue should confess that Jesus Christ is Lord, to the glory of God the Father" (Phil. 2:10–11). If you believe that this passage is asking you to make Jesus Lord of your life, then the entire world will be asked one day to do the same. Are they saved or will they be saved? No! The term Lord in both cases means that you are admitting that Jesus is the Lord. He's Lord over creation and the circumstances of your life. He knows each sparrow that falls and the number of hairs on your head. Jesus is sovereign over all. You can voluntarily admit that Jesus is Lord now or do so later.

There is a second way Jesus is Lord: Jesus is or can be Lord of your life. "I beseech you therefore, brethren, by the mercies of God, that ye present your bodies a living sacrifice, holy, acceptable unto God, which is your reasonable service" (Rom. 12:1). How can anyone other than those already saved present their bodies as living sacrifices? The unsaved are considered dead to God until made alive by the new birth. God will not accept any sacrifice from the unsaved. "The sacrifice of the wicked is an abomination to the Lord" (Prov. 15:8a). A person can't present his body holy until

## CONFLICTING SIGNS CONFUSE SINNERS

after he is saved and has become holy. This passage has to do with Christian service, not salvation.

> Jesus is the Savior of many souls He is not Lord of.

So there are really two ways *Lord* is used. Jesus is the Lord. He is Lord over all creation. He can do as he wants with it. Jesus can also be your Lord if you allow him to have control over your life.

This leads us to another question. Is Jesus completely Lord of your life, or is He partially Lord of your life? I don't think I've met anyone who has made Jesus completely Lord of his or her life. Some people make Him more Lord than others, but it is never complete. Is Jesus Lord over your job, over your home, your car, the TV shows you watch, the music you listen to, and the way you spend your leisure time? So if Jesus is only partially Lord, how could anyone possibly believe in lordship salvation? How much do you need to make Him Lord of to be saved? Would 10 percent of your life be enough? Would 25 percent, 50 percent, or more be required? It doesn't make much sense does it?

## The Two Salvations

Not only are their two ways *Lord* is used, but there are also two salvations for the individual. (Actually there are three salvations when you count the future salvation of all believers' bodies.) "How can that be?" you ask. "If there is only one way to get saved, then how can there be two salvations?" There are actually two parts to salvation or two different types of salvation: the salvation of the soul and the salvation of the life. The soul is what you are. You don't have a soul. You are a soul that has a body. When we are talking about being saved, we are usually talking about the soul (see Rom. 10:13). We are not referring to the body or the life lived in the body. The soul is saved by believing in Christ. It is all God's work. You just receive it. That's your part. Along with salvation of the soul comes the availability or potential for the temporal life to be saved (salvaged). This is largely your work and responsibility. "Work out your own salvation with fear and trembling" (Phil. 2:12b). The salvation of the soul and the salvation of the life are two distinctly different salvations. In Romans 12:1-2, the apostle Paul encouraged believers to transform their lives. Once your soul is saved your life can change also, if you want it to. It's your choice.

Your soul is saved by believing in Christ; your life is saved by obeying Christ when you follow the principles set forth in the Bible. The salvation of the soul is received instantaneously by a single act of faith, while the salvation of a life is a gradual process that is dependent on the degree you are willing to work at it, by continual acts of faith. It is important to understand you can be trusting Jesus' death on the cross to pay your sin debt and not also simultaneously be trusting Him for other things.

God always does a good job of His work. Every soul that has ever been saved still is. There are no degrees of the soul's salvation. It is the same for everyone. Either you are saved or you are not. But in the salvation of a life, man sometimes does not do his job well and may have varying degrees of success. This means that there are believers who live and die in various stages of Christian growth. These range from full complete spiritual maturity to no apparent growth or life salvation at all. Since man is justified in the sight of fellow man by what he does, others judge the salvation of a man's life to determine if he has salvation of the soul. Consequently, everybody who has a saved soul doesn't appear to be saved, but only those who are working on their lives' salvation. In other words, everyone who is going to heaven doesn't act like it.

The line that separates salvation of the soul from salvation of the life is extremely blurred in many churches. What makes this so dangerous is that your works are on one side of the line and God's grace is on the other. It is important to distinguish between them. The following comparison should help you to see the differences between the salvation of the soul (Jesus is your Savior) and the salvation of the life (Jesus is your Lord).

| **Jesus is your Savior** | **Jesus is your Lord** |
| --- | --- |
| Salvation of your soul | Salvation of your life |
| Overcome sin's penalty | Overcome sin's power |
| God was your Judge. | God is now your Father. |
| Permanent, cannot be lost | Conditional, must be sought |
| The Holy Spirit comes in to live (indwelling). | The Holy Spirit is allowed to control (infilling). |
| Justification (instantaneous) | Sanctification (progressive) |
| Peace with God | Peace of God |
| You are born a child of God. | You behave like God's child. |
| The sinner comes to Christ. | The believer comes to usefulness. |
| You are "in Christ." | You are "abiding in Christ." |
| A believer | A disciple |
| Starts a relationship (father/child) | Fellowship occurs. |
| Everlasting life | Abundant life |

## MAKE JESUS LORD OF YOUR LIFE

| | |
|---|---|
| By believing you receive (imputed righteousness) | By obeying you receive (personal righteousness) |
| Justifies man in the sight of God | Justifies man in the sight of man |
| Regeneration—the work of the Holy Spirit | Conversion—the work of the church |
| The sinner becomes a saint. | The saint becomes a servant. |
| You confess belief on Christ to receive. | You confess sins to maintain. |
| You have it because Jesus died for you. | You can have it because Jesus is praying for you. |
| There's a change in your eternal destination. | There's a change in your life. |
| You are going to heaven. | You are determining your rank and privilege in heaven. |
| Your name is written in heaven. | Your deeds are recorded in heaven. |
| You are a new creation. | It becomes apparent to you and to others that you are a new creation. |
| You were in bondage to sin; now you are free to choose. | You make a conscious choice not to sin but to do right. |

People sometimes make statements about the salvation of another person such as, "He got a good dose of salvation," or "She really got saved." They are usually talking about salvation of the soul or both the salvation of the soul and the salvation of the life. These adjectives might accurately describe salvation of the life but should never be used to describe salvation of the soul. Soul salvation is equal for all. Life salvation is relative and is the only one of the two that you can describe in relative terms.

Failing to distinguish between the two salvations has individuals taking the conditions for discipleship and making them prerequisites for salvation of the soul. There is already enough confusion about the role humans play in salvation. Don't add to the confusion by failing to distinguish between the two types of salvation.

## The Good Shepherd

John 10:9–10b says, "I am the door: by me if any man enter in, he shall be saved, and shall go in and out, and find pasture. . . I am come that they might have life and that they might have it more abundantly." You obtain everlasting life by entering the door of the sheepfold. After you have entered the door, you are able to obtain an abundant temporal life to whatever degree you are willing to go in and out and find pasture. You can keep an abundant life as long as you are willing to continue going out to pasture. The pasture represents prayer, Bible study, church attendance, witnessing, giving, etc. All of these things will help a Christian to have an abundant life. In other words, I'm going to heaven because I entered the door of the sheepfold. I can also have heaven here on earth to whatever degree I'm willing to follow the Shepherd. If I enter the door and never look for pasture or follow the Shepherd, I'm still going to heaven. If following the Shepherd and finding pasture were both essential to salvation, then God would have written, "If any man enter in and find pasture, he shall be saved." I don't follow the Shepherd to get Him to save me or keep me saved; I enter the door to be saved. Then I follow the Shepherd in gratitude because He's already saved me.

The Shepherd stands at the door and beckons the lost to enter. He does not say, "Only the lost that are willing to follow me out to pasture and back to the fold may enter.

The rest of you may stay lost until you become willing to follow." The Shepherd has everlasting life to *give* to those who will trust Him, not everlasting life to *trade* with those who will follow Him.

Unfortunately some of the sheep stand by the door and distort the Shepherd's call, saying, "The Shepherd said you couldn't enter unless you promise to follow once you're inside." Other sheep standing by the door tell those who are thinking of entering the fold, "You can't be saved unless you repent of a life of grazing in bad pasture and promise to graze in good pasture." Is it possible for sheep to enter the door and be saved before they even learn that following the Shepherd is a choice available on the other side?

Sometimes the sheep in the fold have made salvation unobtainable for other sheep. Some of them standing by the door are wolves dressed as sheep. They keep souls from entering by adding works to grace. Those that performed works in order to enter may think they are saved when they may not be. If you make a promise to follow or to give up your bad pastures, you are not entering by the door. You are *observing* the door then attempting to go around it by making a *trade*.

It is foolish to think one can obtain everlasting life by promising to improve the temporal life. However, if you could obtain everlasting life by promising to follow after entering, then it makes sense that you could lose it when you failed to hold up your end of the bargain.

It is worth noting that the door to everlasting life swings one way: *In*. The door to abundant life is not the door to everlasting life but rather it is inside the door to everlasting life. The door to abundant life swings both ways: *In* and *Out*. You can have it and then lose it. You must work to keep it, but you can't even qualify for it until you enter the door to everlasting salvation.

# CONFLICTING SIGNS CONFUSE SINNERS

Sheep may enter the fold for different reasons. Some may be drawn to the door of salvation because of the pasture-finding benefit. They may say to themselves, "My life is out of control. I'll get saved and let God control it." Then there are other sheep who may not know of the pasture-finding benefits who say, "If I can be saved by entering the door, then I'm going to do it."

Be careful of sheep inspectors. They see one of God's sheep struggling to find pasture or lying in the fold not even looking for pasture and say, "He doesn't live the life, so he probably never really entered the door." Be careful, the fellow you think is living the life might be trusting his pasture-finding ability to get him to heaven.

## Sheep Court

| | |
|---|---|
| Bailiff: | All rise. The sheepfold court will now come to order. The honorable judge Faithful Sheep presiding. |
| Judge: | Thank you, you may be seated. Court is now in session. Case #SX-338-592: The Flock vs. Stray Sheep. Prosecution, are you ready to present your case? |
| Prosecution: | We are, Your Honor. |
| Judge: | Defense, do you wish to enter a plea at this time? |
| Defense: | Not guilty, Your Honor. |
| Judge: | Prosecution, you may call your first witness. |
| Prosecution: | We would like to call Mr. Curly Wool Carl to the stand. |

| | |
|---|---|
| Bailiff: | Mr. Carl, do you swear to tell the truth, the whole, truth, and nothing but the truth, so help you God? |
| Curly Wool Carl: | I do. |
| Judge: | You may take the stand, Mr. Carl. |
| Prosecution: | Mr. Carl, have you ever observed any violations of the fold contract by Stray Sheep? |
| Curly Wool Carl: | Yes. Last Thursday, Stray Sheep did not arise until 6:30 A.M. She missed being led out to pasture by the shepherd and stayed in the sheepfold all day. |
| Prosecution: | Mr. Carl, have you observed any other violations of the fold contract by Stray Sheep? |
| Curly Wool Carl: | Yes. Stray sheep hasn't had her wool trimmed in weeks and I heard she hasn't been giving 10 percent of her wool to the general fold fund. |
| Defense: | Objection. That's hearsay. |
| Judge: | Sustained. |
| Prosecution: | Thank you Mr. Carl. The prosecution has no more questions for this witness. |
| Judge: | Defense, do you want to cross examine? |
| Defense: | We do you honor. Mr. Carl, how do you know that Stray Sheep got up late on the day in question? |
| Curly Wool Carl: | I was having my wool trimmed at the Cutting Corner, when Stray Sheep came out of pen #6. |

# CONFLICTING SIGNS CONFUSE SINNERS

Defense: Mr. Carl, why were you still in the fold?

Curly Wool Carl: I never go to pasture on Thursdays. That's when I have my wool trimmed and styled. It's so hard to get an appointment in the evening.

Defense: Thank you Mr. Carl. No more questions.

Judge: Bailiff, please take Mr. Carl to the holding cell. By his own admission, he is in violation of the fold contract.

Defense: We would like to call Stray Sheep to the stand.

Bailiff: Ms. Stray, do you swear to tell the truth, the whole truth and nothing but the truth, so help you God?

Stray Sheep: I do.

Judge: You may take the stand, Ms. Stray.

Defense: Is it true that your wool hasn't been trimmed lately?

Stray Sheep: It's true. I've been infected with wool lice and none of the shearers will come anywhere near me.

Defense: I see. Is it also true that last Thursday you got up late and did not go out to pasture?

Stray Sheep: Yes, I was sick the night before, and I overslept.

Defense: Thank you Ms. Stray. I have no more questions.

Judge: Prosecution, do you wish to cross examine?

| | |
|---|---|
| Prosecution: | We do, Your Honor. Ms. Stray, did you fill out an irregular shearing slip? |
| Stray Sheep: | What's that? I've never heard of it. |
| Prosecution: | If you'd read your wool production manual faithfully, you'd be aware of all the flock policies and procedures. Ms. Stray, did you report to the Sheep Medical Center when you were taken ill? |
| Stray Sheep: | No, I was too sick, and none of the rest of the members of the flock would help me get there. |
| Prosecution: | I have no more questions, Your Honor. |
| Judge: | You may step down Ms. Stray. Prosecution, you may make your closing arguments. |
| Prosecution: | Thank you, Your Honor. Ladies and gentlemen of the jury, as you can see, Stray Sheep is bringing reproach on our sheepfold. She is sickly, irresponsible, and infected with wool lice. She may soon infect all of us. The only responsible thing to do is to remove her from the fold immediately. We cannot have the likes of her ruining our reputations. Please do your duty to protect us all by expelling Stray Sheep from the fold. Thank you. |
| Judge: | Defense, you may make your closing arguments. |
| Defense: | Thank you, Your Honor. Ladies and gentlemen of the jury, Stray Sheep is a new arrival to our fold. It will take |

|  |  |
|---|---|
|  | her time to learn all of the policies and procedures. It is our responsibility to reach out and love our neighbors. Please have compassion for Stray Sheep. Thank you. |
| Judge: | Jurors, you have the responsibility for determining if Ms. Stray Sheep is guilty of violating her fold contract. I caution you to take your job seriously. You are to carefully consider all the evidence and be in complete agreement before you can announce a verdict. You are now dismissed to the deliberation room. |
|  | ...jury deliberation... |
| Judge: | Jurors, have you reached a verdict? |
| Jury Foreman: | We have, your honor. |
| Judge: | Stray Sheep, would you please rise? How does the Jury rule in the case of The Flock vs. Stray Sheep? |
| Jury Foreman: | We find the defendant guilty. |
| Judge: | Stray sheep, the jury has found you guilty of violating the policies and procedures of the fold contract. You are hereby sentenced to permanent expulsion from the sheepfold effective immediately. Bailiff, would you please have Ms. Stray get her things and then escort her to the gate of the fold. |
| **Shepherd:** | Break it up guys, no more games tonight. It's time for bed. |

# MAKE JESUS LORD OF YOUR LIFE

**Sunday's Only: 2 for 1 Sale!**
Get both the salvation of your soul and the salvation of your life for the price of one!!!

If you understand that there are two different types of salvation then you will be able to appreciate the two for one sale comic. Eternal salvation of the soul is completely free because Jesus paid the price. Complete temporal salvation of the life is very expensive; it will cost your life. For many Christians this is too difficult to handle. They feel that salvation of the soul is too inexpensive and that salvation of the life is too costly. So what do they do? They put them together and offer a package deal. This makes it palatable for both the buyer and seller. The seller (soul-winner) doesn't want to sell anyone something that's free and the buyer (unsaved individual) doesn't want to accept something that doesn't cost anything.

## WRONG ROUTE #12
......................................
# SAY THE SINNER'S PRAYER

Pastor: This morning I would like everyone who walked down the aisle for salvation, to repeat this prayer after me:

> Dear Jesus
> I know that I'm a sinner.
> I believe that You died for me.
> I believe that You were buried for me.
> I believe that You rose from the dead for me.
> I believe that You are sitting at the right hand of God for me.
> I believe that You're coming back for me.
> I repent of my sins right now.
> I turn from my sins.
> I confess my sins.
> I ask you to forgive my sins.
> I give my whole heart to you right now.
> I promise I will live for you.
> I promise I will serve you.
> Right now, I make you Lord of my life.

# CONFLICTING SIGNS CONFUSE SINNERS

> I promise I'll witness for you.
> I promise I'll read my Bible and pray every day.
> I promise I'll attend every church service.
> Please save me!
> Amen.

THE SINNER'S PRAYER has been developed in recent years in order to make it more convenient to get people saved and to make sinners feel more comfortable. It can be prayed on an individual basis, repeated after another person, or even recited as a congregation. It goes something like this:

> Dear Jesus, I know that I'm a sinner. I am sorry for my sins, please forgive me. I believe that you died for me. With all of my heart I now turn from my sins and receive you as my Savior. I'm going to live for you from now on. Amen.

There are several things that are generally thought to be necessary as part of a sinner's prayer. These include: admitting that you are a sinner, expressing sorrow for your sins, acknowledging that Jesus died for you, asking Jesus to come into your heart, turning from your sins, and committing your life to Him. Of course many variations exist, but most sinner's prayers contain several of the above.

The sinner's prayer or a variation of it has been prayed by millions of individuals who desire to be saved. There are several potential problems with this approach. First, it causes people to focus on the words being prayed, not on complete trust in Christ. Secondly, some individuals may be distracted by those around them who are reciting the same prayer. Finally, reciting a sinner's prayer may cause some individuals to say words they do not even mean or understand. The prayer doesn't save you; it should simply be an expression of one's complete trust in Jesus as Savior.

As a soul-winner, I (Trent) would first give a clear presentation of the gospel. If the person is willing to trust Christ, then, I would lead him or her in a prayer to tell Christ that the person is now placing complete trust in Him for salvation. In this case it is helpful for a sinner to repeat a prayer after the soul-winner, but only after he or she has heard a clear explanation of what it means to trust in Jesus. A prayer used in this manner works best in a one-on-one or small group setting. This is an effective way to use a sinner's prayer.

Romans 10:9 says, "That if thou shalt confess with thy mouth the Lord Jesus, and shalt believe in thine heart that God hath raised him from the dead, thou shalt be saved." In Romans 10:13 we read, "For whosoever shall call upon the name of the Lord shall be saved." There is no mention in either verse of a sinner's prayer. If we call on the name of the Lord, we are asking Him to save us. If we confess the Lord Jesus, we are confessing that He is our Savior.

The sinner's prayer doesn't save you. Telling Jesus that you are turning from your sins, feeling sorry for your sins, or committing to live for Christ won't save you either. Only complete trust in Christ can save you.

# PART 2

# THE ONE WAY TO SALVATION

CHAPTER 13

# UNDERSTANDING SALVATION

WHILE THE BULK of this book deals with wrong applications of salvation, you may still have many questions about salvation. This chapter will answer many of them.

## What do we mean when we say that someone has been saved?

John 5:24 says, "Verily, verily, I say unto you, He that heareth my word, and believeth on him that sent me, hath everlasting life, and shall not come into condemnation; but is passed from death unto life." When we trust in Jesus, we are saved from the condemnation that results in spending eternity in hell.

## Why do I need to be saved?

You need to be saved because you are lost. "For the Son of man is come to seek and to save that which was lost" (Luke 19:10). The reason you are lost is because you were born a sinner. "For as by one man's disobedience many were made sinners, so by the obedience of one shall many be made righteous" (Rom. 5:19). Adam is the man whose disobedience made us all sinners. Jesus is the man whose obedience will make many righteous.

## How do I get saved?

To get saved, do as the Bible states and place your complete trust in Jesus Christ for salvation:

> That if thou shalt confess with thy mouth the Lord Jesus, and shalt believe in thine heart that God hath raised him from the dead, thou shalt be saved. For with the heart man believeth unto righteousness; and with the mouth confession is made unto salvation.
> (Rom. 10:9–10)

> Sirs, what must I do to be saved? And they said, Believe on the Lord Jesus Christ, and thou shalt be saved, and thy house.
> (Acts 16:30b–31)

## Can I do anything to earn salvation?

No. "But we are all as an unclean thing, and all our righteousnesses are as filthy rags" (Isa. 64:6a). "For by grace are ye saved through faith; and that not of yourselves: it is the gift of God: Not of works, lest any man should boast" (Eph. 2:8–9).

## Do I have to give up anything to get saved?

A person is saved by believing on the Lord Jesus Christ. To believe is to completely trust in Jesus for salvation. The only thing that a person needs to give up is false belief or unbelief.

## What part of me is saved?

The soul and spirit are the parts of us that are saved. Your soul is your mind, will, and emotions. Your spirit is your inner being. The only part of you that is not saved is your physical body. When you die, your body will be buried, but your soul and spirit will go to heaven.

## When do I get saved?

We are saved the moment we trust Christ. "He that believeth on the Son hath everlasting life" (John 3:36a). Notice the word *hath,* which is in the present tense. You receive salvation the moment you believe on Christ.

## Am I permanently saved, or will I only be certain when I make it to heaven?

Once you trust Christ you are completely saved. You can be certain now because God is as good as His Word. He cannot lie. Titus 1:2 says, "In hope of eternal life, which God, that cannot lie, promised before the world began." If God promised salvation before the world began, you can be certain your salvation is permanent.

## Am I saved from sinning again?

No. "If we say that we have not sinned, we make him a liar, and his word is not in us" (1 John 1:10). That includes everyone who is saved, because the book of 1 John was written to believers, not to unbelievers.

## Am I only saved from my past sins?

No. Since Jesus bore all our sins in his own body on the cross, all of our sins were paid for by his death. When Jesus died on the cross, all of our sins were in the future. The moment we trust Christ we are saved from the penalty of all of our sins: past, present, and future. "And the Lord hath laid on him [Christ] the iniquity of us all" (Isa. 53:6b, author's insertion).

## What should I do when I sin after I've been saved?

Confess them. "If we confess our sins, he is faithful and just to forgive us our sins, and to cleanse us from all unrighteousness" (1 John 1:9).

## If God forgave my sins when I was saved, why do I need to confess my sins after I am saved?

Sin or disobedience separates the believer from fellowship with his Heavenly Father. It does not break the relationship with the Father. Confessing our sins to Him restores fellowship. The consequence of sin in the life of a believer will bring chastisement if he does not judge himself. Chastisement is child training. The consequence of sin in the life of a believer will never be condemnation. "For if we would judge ourselves, we should not be judged. But when we are judged, we are chastened of the Lord, that we should not be condemned with the world" (1 Cor. 11:31–32).

## Can I get saved if I have some bad habits that I can't get rid of?

Yes, the only thing you need to give up to get saved is unbelief.

## What if I can't give up my bad habits after I'm saved?

When you are saved from sin's penalty you gain access to the power to overcome bad habits. "I beseech you therefore, brethren, by the mercies of God, that ye present your bodies a living sacrifice, holy, acceptable unto God, which is your reasonable service. And be not conformed to this world: but be ye transformed by the renewing of your mind, that ye may prove what is that good, and acceptable, and perfect, will of God" (Rom. 12:1–2). The more you give of yourself to God, the easier it will become to break bad habits.

## Does Jesus keep me saved, or am I responsible?

We are kept by the power of God. "Blessed be the God and Father of our Lord Jesus Christ, which according to his abundant mercy hath begotten us again unto a lively hope by the resurrection of Jesus Christ from the dead, To an inheritance incorruptible, and undefiled, and that fadeth not away, reserved in heaven for you, Who are kept by the power of God through faith unto salvation ready to be revealed in the last time" (1 Peter 1:3–5).

## Can anything take away my salvation?

No. "And I give unto them eternal life; and they shall never perish, neither shall any man pluck them out of my hand" (John 10:28). "For I am persuaded, that neither death, nor life, nor angels, nor principalities, nor powers, nor things present, nor things to come, Nor height, nor depth, nor any other creature, shall be able to separate us from the love of God, which is in Christ Jesus our Lord" (Rom. 8:38–39).

## What are the benefits of salvation?

The major benefit of salvation is eternal life. This means that when you die you go to heaven to live with Jesus forever. The other benefits of salvation could be summed up using the term *abundant life*. When you give different parts of your life to God—like your finances, marriage,

# UNDERSTANDING SALVATION

children, time, etc.—God will bless these areas and you will experience the abundant life.

## Do I have to do anything to receive the benefits that accompany salvation?

Yes, the only thing that is automatically and absolutely free and complete about salvation is eternal life. Your salvation entitles you to other benefits, all of which have requirements for receipt. For example, to receive God's benefits for your marriage, you will need to find out what the Bible says about marriage and incorporate those principles into your life.

## What happens if I do not trust Christ for salvation?

Failure to trust Christ as Savior will result in condemnation remaining on the unbeliever. This condemnation will result in eternal punishment in the lake of fire.

> He that believeth on him is not condemned: but he that believeth not is condemned already, because he hath not believed in the name of the only begotten Son of God.
> 
> (John 3:18)

> And I saw the dead, small and great, stand before God; and the books were opened: and another book was opened, which is the book of life: and the dead were judged out of those things which were written in the books, according to their works. And the sea gave up the dead which were in it; and death and hell delivered up the dead which were in them: and they were judged every man according to their works. And death and hell were cast into the lake of fire. This is the second death.

And whosoever was not found written in the book of life was cast into the lake of fire.

(Rev. 20:12–15)

## How can a loving God punish anyone?

God is a God of love, but He is also a God of justice. Sin separates us from God. Since God is holy, anyone who does not trust in Christ as Savior cannot be in the presence of God but is condemned to hell. When we trust in Jesus, He becomes our righteousness, and then we can be in the presence of God.

## How can I know that I'm saved?

The basis of assurance of salvation is the written Word of God. "These things have I written unto you that believe on the name of the Son of God; that ye may know that ye have eternal life, and that ye may believe on the name of the Son of God" (1 John 5:13). "The Spirit itself beareth witness with our spirit, that we are the children of God" (Rom. 8:16).

## How can I tell if someone else is saved?

We often look at a person's lifestyle to determine if he or she is saved. But remember, there are many carnal Christians and some unbelievers live very moral lives. A better method would be to listen to what a person says. If they say they are depending on Jesus to give them salvation, then they are saved. If they are depending on things other than Jesus, they are either unsaved or saved but confused.

UNDERSTANDING SALVATION

## Is it important to tell other people about salvation?

Yes. The only way people can learn how to be saved is if others who are saved tell them. "How then shall they call on him in whom they have not believed? and how shall they believe in him of whom they have not heard? and how shall they hear without a preacher? And how shall they preach, except they be sent? as it is written, How beautiful are the feet of them that preach the gospel of peace, and bring glad tidings of good things!" (Rom. 10:14–15).

## Is there more to Christianity than just salvation?

Certainly. You should experience the abundant life that Jesus has to offer us. The Bible contains an answer for any problem we could experience. If you will do what it says, you will experience the blessings that it promises.

In order to gain a further understanding of salvation, you should understand how the roles of Adam and Jesus relate to each other. "For since by man came death, by man came also the resurrection of the dead. For as in Adam all die, even so in Christ shall all be made alive. . . And so it is written, The first man Adam, was made a living soul; the last Adam was made a quickening spirit" (1 Cor. 15:21, 22, 45).

The following table parallels the first Adam with the last Adam (Jesus):

| Adam | Jesus |
| --- | --- |
| Head of the human race | Head of the spirit race |
| The son of God (created) | The Son of God (eternal) |

## CONFLICTING SIGNS CONFUSE SINNERS

| | |
|---|---|
| Had no human father | Had no human father |
| Caused eternal death to pass upon all men when they were born physically | Responsible for eternal life which is given to all men when they are born again spiritually. |

The sin penalty (eternal death) is imposed upon man automatically because of Adam's sin. You were born a sinner because you inherited a sin nature. You are not a sinner because of your conduct. God forgives the sin penalty and grants eternal life to man automatically when he is born again spiritually by placing all of his trust in Christ for salvation. You are a saint because of your new nature (spiritual birth).

# CHAPTER 14

## to Heaven!

**B**Y THIS TIME you're probably wondering what you should do to get saved. Well let's see what we've learned:

- You can't get saved by repenting of your sins, and you can't receive salvation by confessing them.
- Salvation doesn't come by giving up bad habits or by being convicted of them.
- Sorrow over sin won't save you; neither will pleas for forgiveness.
- You can't give away your heart to receive salvation, neither can you live right to keep it.

## CONFLICTING SIGNS CONFUSE SINNERS

- You can't maintain your salvation to make it to glory, nor profess Christ publicly to gain God's favor.
- You won't get saved by following Jesus or by surrendering your life to Him.
- But wait, what about the sinner's prayer? You'd better check out Romans 10:13.

It might look as though there's nothing left. But you need to realize something. All of the various methods of salvation discussed so far were made up by sincere, well-meaning Christians who didn't fully understand what the Bible said or who incorporated their own experience into its plan. Many have been passed down from generation to generation. Where should we look for what's right? Let's go back to the Bible and see what it says.

The following is a list of verses on salvation. We will compare them to see what they have in common:

- In Acts 8:37 the Ethiopian eunuch wanted to be baptized. What criteria does Philip give him? He said, "If thou *believest* with all thine heart, thou mayest." The eunuch responded, "I *believe* that Jesus Christ is the Son of God."
- But as many as received him, to them gave he power to become the sons of God, even to them that *believe* on his name (John 1:12).
- In Acts 16:30b the Philippian jailer asked, "Sirs, what must I do to be saved?" In verse 31 Paul and Silas responded, "*Believe* on the Lord Jesus Christ, and thou shalt be saved, and thy house."
- In I Corinthians 1:21 it says, "For after that in the wisdom of God the world by wisdom knew not God, it pleased God by the foolishness of preaching to save them that *believe.*"
- For God so loved the world, that he gave his only begotten Son, that whosoever *believeth* in him should not perish, but have everlasting life. (John 3:16)
- In John 3:36 we read: "He that *believeth* on the Son hath everlasting life: and he that *believeth* not the Son shall not see life, but the wrath of God abideth on him."

(Author's emphasis throughout)

What ties all these verses together? It is the word *believe*. So simple, yet so complicated. We need to believe on Jesus for our salvation. This involves completely trusting in Him and not in our own righteousness or works. That's it. There's no more. Receiving salvation is that simple. That's why so many people miss it.

## Biblical Examples of Believing

What does it mean to believe in Christ? In James 2:19 we read, "Thou *believest* that there is one God; thou doest well:

the devils also *believe*, and tremble." Are the devil and his demons saved? No. They know that Jesus is God and that He has the power to judge them. That is why they "tremble." In order to better understand what it means to believe we can look at other salvation verses that use different words:

- Romans 10:9, 10 says, "That if thou shalt *confess* with thy mouth the Lord Jesus, and shalt believe in thine heart that God hath raised him from the dead, thou shalt be saved. For with the heart man believeth unto righteousness; and with the mouth *confession* is made unto salvation." In this passage believing with the heart followed by a verbal confession brings salvation.
- Romans 10:13 uses a different word. "For whosoever shall *call* upon the name of the Lord shall be saved." In this verse calling on the Lord brings salvation.
- John 1:12 uses "believe" and "receive." "But as many as *received* him, to them gave he power to become the sons of God, even to them that believe on his name."
- In John 10:9 we read, "I am the door: by me if any man *enter in*, he shall be saved, and shall go in and out, and find pasture."
(Author's emphasis throughout)

So what does it mean to believe? Confessing the Lord Jesus, calling on the name of the Lord, receiving Jesus, and entering the door (Jesus) are all different expressions the Bible uses to picture what it means to believe. It is worth noting that all of these are a single act, not a process. If you confess the Lord Jesus, call on the name of the Lord, receive Jesus, or enter the door, you will be saved. You have believed!

ONE WAY TO HEAVEN!

## How much faith is enough?

A logical question to ask about salvation is: How much faith is required to receive it? The amount of trust or faith a sinner has for salvation is not important. It is the OBJECT of their trust that is important. A sinner must place all of his trust in Christ. Nowhere in the Bible is there even a hint of the promise of everlasting life to the individual who doesn't place all of his trust in Christ. In Acts 8:37 Philip responded to the Ethiopian eunuch, "If thou believest with all thine heart, thou mayest."

Jesus is the way, only to the sinner
who is trusting only Him, all the way.
He won't pick up hitchhiking sinners
who are trusting something else
to take them part of the way.

Any individual who, in his quest for salvation, begins with some form of works such as keeping the Ten Commandments, giving money, or turning from sins and then adds on a little bit of belief or trust in Christ for good measure, is going to hell when he dies, just like the individual who has no trust in Christ. You cannot add anything to trust in Christ. He is not a supplement and He won't be supplemented. In John 14:6a Jesus said, "I am the way, the truth, and the life: no man cometh unto the father, but by me." Notice He is not part of the way. It doesn't say, "No man cometh unto the Father but by me and . . ." There is no "and."

## The Narrow Gate

The problem with trusting Jesus alone for salvation comes down to understanding what Jesus meant by the narrow gate. "Enter ye in at the strait (narrow) gate: for wide is the gate, and broad is the way, that leadeth to destruction, and many there be which go in thereat: Because strait is the gate, and narrow is the way, which leadeth unto life, and few there be that find it" (Matt. 7:13–14). Two different things are being described in this passage, the gate and the way. The gate symbolizes salvation, while the way represents a Christian's spiritual walk after salvation. For our purposes here we will only discuss the gate. One gate is strait, or narrow, and the other is wide. It is hard to get through the narrow gate but easy to get through the wide gate. In order to get through the narrow gate, and you must place 100 percent of your trust in Christ for salvation. This is the only way to enter. It is easy to get through the broad gate because you can believe anything. You can place your faith in any cult leader you want. You can follow the false religion of your choice. You can also place some of your faith in your ability to turn from your sins, or in surrendering your life, or in your ability to live the Christian life. Any of these things will do. But it is hard to get through the narrow gate because you must place all of your faith in Jesus to get in.

The best way to sum it all up is with the question the Philippian jailer asked Paul and Silas in Act 16:30b. "Sirs, what must I do to be saved?" In verse 31 they responded, "*Believe* on the Lord Jesus Christ, and thou shalt be saved, and thy house" (author's emphasis).

# CHAPTER 15
## ASSURANCE OF SALVATION

### False-Based Assurance

MANY PEOPLE HAVE a false assurance of their salvation because they base it on the wrong criteria. This often happens because they interpret a scripture verse incorrectly. One commonly misused verse is 1 John 3:14a: "We know that we have passed from death unto life, because we love the brethren." Many individuals believe that they are "passed from death unto life" because they enjoy going to church and fellowshipping with the brethren. The only problem is that the people in false cults love their brethren too. Some people say, "I know I'm saved because there is a change in my life." That may be true, but there are former alcoholics who attend alcoholics support group meetings who also have changed lives.

Others will use the fact that they enjoy reading their Bible as their assurance of salvation. Being "passed from death unto life" is something that happens when a person receives salvation. We go from the kingdom of darkness into the kingdom of light. This may show immediate manifestations, or the effects may be visible later. However, the amount of change in one's life is not a barometer of the assurance of one's salvation.

Another verse people incorrectly base their assurance of salvation on is John 13:35. "By this shall all men know that ye are my disciples, if ye have love one to another." This is not a verse of self-assurance to tell myself that I'm saved. It is not a verse of assurance to let you know that I'm saved. It is not even a verse to let the unsaved know that I'm saved. The purpose of this verse is to let others know that we are disciples of Jesus. Being saved and being a disciple are two different things.

Even non-Christians use scripture to obtain assurance of their "salvation." Some false cults use 2 Timothy 3:12 as an assurance verse. "Yea, and all that will live godly in Christ Jesus shall suffer persecution." Then they go out witnessing, hoping to get cussed out a few times and even have some doors slammed in their faces. This will give them assurance of their "salvation."

> Excuse me sir, I'm trying to get to heaven. Can you help me?
> Hey no problem. Go to the second light, turn left, drive about ½ mile.
> It will be on your right. You can't miss it!

Those who were told to turn from their sins before they could trust Christ for their salvation must get their assurance from whether or not their life is changed. They judge their salvation by their own action. I've (Trent) known false cult members who for years have never doubted their "salvation." But some of the best Baptist soul-winners I've known, have turned back momentarily to a sin they once gave up. What do you suppose they felt they had to do then? They went forward at invitation time and got "really" saved. They probably said something like this: "I'm going to really repent of my sin this time so I'll really be saved." If they trusted Christ in the first place, that's all that will ever be necessary.

It is important to remember that "we walk by faith, not by sight" (2 Cor. 5:7). We should stop inspecting our own and everybody else's fruit (actions) to determine the status of their salvation. But rather we should be looking at the root. That root is what we believe. Is 100 percent of your trust in Jesus? Or does some of your trust for salvation lie in something else?

## True Assurance

True assurance has two aspects, objective and subjective. For the last thirty years I (Trent) have been saved. I don't remember ever doubting my salvation, even for a minute. Why? Because the *only* basis for the assurance of my salvation has been the written Word. I know I'm saved because the Bible says so. I love the brethren, the church, and the Word, but my love or joy doesn't tell me I'm saved. It might tell you I'm saved, after my lips have told you I'm completely trusting Christ as my only hope for heaven. This is the objective part of the assurance of our salvation, because we base it on His promise of salvation to those who believe on Him.

Every Christian needs assurance of his salvation. This should come from God's Word. Let's start with John 3:16. "For God so loved the world, that he gave his only begotten Son, that whosoever believeth in him should not perish, but have everlasting life." Do you believe in the Son? Then you will not perish but you now have everlasting life. In John

3:36a we read, "He that believeth on the Son hath everlasting life." Again, did you believe on the Son? Then you have everlasting life. Romans 10:13 says, "For whosoever shall call upon the name of the Lord shall be saved." Have you called upon the name of the Lord to save you? Then you are saved.

In addition to the written Word we have an internal witness. This is the subjective part. In 1 John 5:13a we read, "These things have I written unto you that believe on the name of the Son of God; that ye may know that ye have eternal life." In verse 10a it says, "He that believeth on the Son of God hath the witness in himself." Who is the witness? The Holy Spirit. The Holy Spirit dwells inside every believer. He should give us assurance of our salvation. Romans 8:16 also indicates that this is how we should know we are God's children. "The Spirit itself beareth witness with our spirit, that we are the children of God." How does this inner witness manifest? He brings to remembrance the Word and confirms the Word. Here's how He does it: When we read verses of assurance, the Holy Spirit inside of us tells us its true. Believe it.

Don't get assurance of your salvation because you have a changed life. Know that you're a child of God because you have believed in Jesus and the Word says you're God's child. Then you will have the Holy Spirit as an inner witness to tell you that you are God's child. The Holy Spirit, who authored the Scriptures, will confirm to you that you can totally rely on God's promises because He guarantees your salvation.

## Can I Lose My Salvation?

No. "And I give unto them eternal life; and they shall never perish, neither shall any man pluck them out of my hand" (John 10:28). How long does everlasting life last? It

## ASSURANCE OF SALVATION

lasts forever. How can you have everlasting life and then lose it?

> You will never have
> the deep abiding peace
> Christ wants you to have
> if you believe
> you could lose your salvation.

Nothing can take away your salvation. "For I am persuaded, that neither death, nor life, nor angels, nor principalities, nor powers, or things present, nor things to come, Nor height, nor depth, nor any other creature, shall be able to separate us from the love of God, which is in Christ Jesus, our Lord" (Rom. 8:38–39).

# PART 3

# WINNING OTHERS TO CHRIST

## CHAPTER 16

# PRAY FOR POWER

WHEN IT COMES to winning others to Christ, the most important thing you can pray for is God's power on you as you witness. "But ye shall receive power, after that the Holy Ghost is come upon you: and ye shall be my witnesses unto me both in Jerusalem, and in all Judaea, and in Samaria, and unto the uttermost part of the earth" (Acts 1:8). The Holy Spirit who lives inside you wants to completely control you, so pray and tell the Holy Spirit that you yield to Him and that you claim His power to lead the lost the Christ. Don't go soul winning without the power of the Holy Spirit.

When you are out witnessing, use your time wisely. Remember that every person you see is a soul for whom Christ died. Every person is going to either heaven or hell when he or she dies. For example, if you stop at a gas station on the way to where you are going to visit, have gospel tracts and be prepared to witness there too. You can't give the plan of salvation to the wrong person.

## CONFLICTING SIGNS CONFUSE SINNERS

As you begin to share the plan of salvation with someone, remember the role God plays in saving the lost. Jesus said, "No man can come to me, except the Father which hath sent me draw him" (John 6:44a). Not only does the Father draw people to Jesus, but He also opens their hearts to receive the gospel. "And a certain woman named Lydia, a seller of purple, of the city of Thyatira, which worshipped God, heard us: whose heart the Lord opened, that she attended unto the things which were spoken of Paul" (Acts 16:14). Once God has opened a person's heart, He shines the light in. "For God, who commanded the light to shine out of darkness, hath shined in our hearts, to give the light of the knowledge of the glory of God in the face of Jesus Christ" (2 Cor. 4:6). Sometimes the Holy Spirit goes ahead of you and prepares the hearts of those He knows you'll be sharing the gospel with. If the Holy Spirit doesn't go ahead of you, He goes with you and begins drawing and preparing hearts as you witness (see Rom. 10:14-17).

It should encourage you to remember that Jesus said, "The harvest truly is great, but the labourers are few: pray ye therefore the Lord of the harvest, that he would send forth labourers into his harvest" (Luke 10:2). This seems to indicate that there are more lost souls who would trust Christ as Savior than there are laborers to share the gospel with them.

You have a guarantee. Yes, God promises that if you sow the seed (the gospel) and encourage lost sinners to trust Christ, you can see immediate results. (see 2 Cor. 6:1-2.) Although not everyone who is given the plan of salvation will trust Christ as his or her Savior, you should expect everyone to do so.

We have clear commands in the scriptures that tell us to go teach the gospel of Christ to the lost. "Go ye therefore, and teach all nations" (Matt. 28:19a). Also consider Mark 16:15, Luke 24:46-48, and Acts 1:8. We therefore do not need some special Holy Spirit leading to go witnessing. So pray and yield yourself to the control of the Holy Spirit. Ask for His power. Claim His fullness, and go believing and expecting to lead lost souls to Christ.

# CHAPTER 17

# MOTIVATION FOR SOUL-WINNING

**Pastor:** This week we will be having special revival services with Evangelist Jim Smith. These will be from Sunday through Thursday at 7:00 P.M. In order to motivate you to bring unsaved friends, we will be giving away some very special prizes. These include a complete Bible concordance, a Bible dictionary, and a set of commentaries on the entire New Testament. So invite your friends and neighbors. Let's pack those pews.

## How to Clean Up Your Life

HOW DO YOU salvage your life after you have trusted Christ completely for salvation? One way is to go soul-winning. Your life will be abundant and full to the degree that you obey Christ in this matter of soul-winning.

Proverbs 11:30 states, "The fruit of the righteous is a tree of life and he that winneth souls is wise." In John 15:16a, Jesus says, "Ye have not chosen me, but I have chosen you, and ordained you, that ye should go and bring forth fruit, and that your fruit should remain." The word *go* in this verse indicates that you have to go get the fruit. So that must mean souls. We should expect to see results because the fruit should remain.

If you are waiting for your life to become clean so you can bear fruit, maybe you should instead bear fruit so your life can become clean. Jesus said in John 15:1–2, "I am the true vine, and my Father is the husbandman. Every branch in me that beareth not fruit he taketh away: and every branch that beareth fruit, he purgeth it, that it may bring forth more fruit." Your Heavenly Father will help you clean up your life as you bear fruit. The fruit of a Christian is not love, joy, peace, etc.; that's the fruit of the Spirit as you yield to the Spirit's control. The fruit of a Christian is other souls that you have led to Christ. Of course, the fruit of the Spirit is a useful tool as we go soul-winning, but we need to make sure that we are not getting sidelined by just being good. Being good is good, but being good so that we can *do* good is better. The fruit of the Spirit should not be the end, but rather the means to an end: winning souls.

Do you want to get victory over a cigarette habit? Go soul-winning! Do you have a problem with gossip? Go soul-winning. When you bear fruit, it will break the bondage of bad habits. So go soul-winning!

Perhaps you've heard "God won't use a dirty vessel." Preachers use this expression to motivate their people to clean up their lives. But according to John 15:1–2 God won't purge (cleanse) the branch that won't bear fruit or yield to usefulness. Maybe we ought to change the expression to "God won't cleanse a dormant vessel much." Soul-winning and separation go hand in hand. The woman at the well in John, chapter 4 received Christ and immediately went soul-winning. She brought a whole town to Christ before she even began to clean up her own life. Get busy soul-winning so God can get busy giving you victory over your bad habits.

Your soul is saved when you become a *believer*. Your life is saved when you become a *follower*. Faith cleans up your soul, while following cleans up your life. In Matthew 4:19, Jesus said, "Follow me, and I will make you fishers of men." Personal soul-winning is your opportunity to help clean up your life.

## Gospel-Hardened or Gospel-Ignorant?

Some people don't see the need to go soul-winning because they think that everyone has already heard the gospel. They reason that since the gospel has been heard and rejected, that most people are gospel-hardened. The truth is that society is not gospel-hardened, but rather gospel-ignorant. An individual who hears and understands how to be saved but neglects or rejects salvation will immediately lose his or her understanding of how to be saved. "When any one heareth the word of the kingdom, and understandeth it not, then cometh the wicked one, and catcheth away that which was sown in his heart. This is he which received seed by the way side" (Matt. 13:19). Another reason to go soul-winning is to plant more seeds, since the devil stole the seeds that did not take root the first time.

## Why Should We Go Soul-Winning?

In addition to helping you clean up your life, the major motivation for soul winning is to see the lost saved. Let's look closely at this. First of all, recognize that salvation can be found only in Jesus. "Neither is there salvation in any other: for there is none other name under heaven given among men, whereby we must be saved" (Acts 4:12). "For

## CONFLICTING SIGNS CONFUSE SINNERS

there is one God, and one mediator between God and men, the man Christ Jesus" (1 Tim. 2:5).

Jesus also commanded us to go and teach the gospel. "Go ye therefore, and teach all nations, baptizing them in the name of the Father, and of the Son, and of the Holy Ghost: Teaching them to observe all things whatsoever I have commanded you: and, lo, I am with you always, even unto the end of the world. Amen" (Matt. 28:19–20). The only way anyone will hear is if we go tell them. "How then shall they call on him in whom they have not believed? and how shall they believe in him of whom they have not heard? and how shall they hear without a preacher" (Rom. 10:14)?

You should also remember than anyone who doesn't accept Christ will go to hell. "And whosoever was not found written in the book of life was cast into the lake of fire" (Rev. 20:15). Hell is a terrible place.

> And it came to pass, that the beggar died, and was carried by the angels into Abraham's bosom: the rich man also died, and was buried; And in hell he lift up his eyes, being in torments, and seeth Abraham afar off, and Lazarus in his bosom. And he cried and said, Father Abraham, have mercy on me, and send Lazarus, that he may dip the tip of his finger in water, and cool my tongue: for I am tormented in this flame.
> (Luke 16:22-24)

> And if thy hand offend thee, cut it off: it is better for thee to enter into life maimed, than having two hands, to go into hell, into the fire that never shall be quenched . . . Where their worm dieth not, and the fire is not quenched.
> (Mark 9:43,44,46)

Hell doesn't sound like a very nice place to be, does it?

## MOTIVATION FOR SOUL-WINNING

The final motivation is for Christians. We will be judged according to our works. Our most important mandate is to witness to the lost. (see Luke 19:10; John 20:21.) It we neglect to do this, can we hope to escape God's judgment? "For we must all appear before the judgment seat of Christ, that every one may receive the things done in his body, according to that he hath done, whether it be good or bad" (2 Cor. 5:10). In addition to being judged for what we have done, we will be rewarded. "And, behold, I come quickly, and my reward is with me, to give every man according as his work shall be" (Rev. 22:12).

Charles Stanley has written in more detail what awaits the Christian for eternity.[1]

The consequences of being an unfruitful Christian won't end at the judgment seat of Christ. It is there where your rank and privilege in Christ's earthly kingdom and later in God's eternal kingdom will be determined. Your service to Christ or lack thereof has eternal consequences. So get busy.

CHAPTER 18

# DOOR-TO-DOOR EVANGELISM

## Where Should I Go Soul-Winning?

**Y**OU CAN LEAD a person to Christ anywhere. However, when you plan to go soul-winning, some places are preferable to others. You may also find certain methods to be better than others, depending on where you live. Remember what the apostle Paul said in 1 Corinthians 9:19-22:

> For though I be free from all men, yet have I made myself servant unto all, that I might gain the more. And unto the Jews I became as a Jew, that I might gain the Jews; to them that are under the law, as under the law, that I might gain them that are under the law; To them that are without law, as without law (being not without law to God, but under the law to Christ,) that I might gain them that are without law. To the weak became I as weak, that I might gain the weak: I am made all things to all men, that I might by all means save some.

The authors have found witnessing to persons in their own homes to be one effective location, because we are talking to people on their own turf. People feel comfortable in their own homes, and they tend to be less preoccupied than they may be elsewhere.

## Getting in the Door

When you plan to share the gospel in people's homes the most critical part of your visit is getting in the door. Dressing appropriately will help. Be aware that a pressed white shirt or blouse, black pants or skirt, and dark tie may signal a type of visit that many people don't want. It is probably best to wear nice casual clothing. It is also important to take along a New Testament small enough to fit in a pocket or purse. Taking along the ten-pound family Bible will likely cause you some problems.

When someone answers the door, the first words out of your mouth are very important. You should tell the individual that you are out visiting from your church. It might not be a good idea to mention the name of the church. Words like Baptist and Pentecostal have a way of turning many people off. You can say it's the church in the neighborhood or the one just down the street instead. You may feel this is being deceptive, but your real goal should not be to boost your own church attendance but rather to win souls to Christ. Next, you should tell the person you would like to visit for a few minutes.

> The 120 prayed until the Spirit empowered them.
> Then they went out to preach about Jesus.
> They didn't hold a service inside
> and invite the sinners to come.

After you've told the person that you'd like to visit, he or she has two choices. If the person lets you in, then you're all set. If the person doesn't let you in, then keep trying. Many common responses to a visit include:

> "I'm on the phone long distance."
> "We're just sitting down to dinner."
> "I was just getting ready to leave for work" or
> "We attend such-and-such church."

The last one is probably the most commonly used excuse and is one of the easiest to overcome. When you receive that response, tell the person that you're not out trying to recruit members or collect donations.

If reasoning with the person doesn't get you in the door, ask if there's a time when you can come back. You can suggest some times. Based on their responses, it becomes fairly easy to tell if a person has any interest whatsoever in talking to you. You won't get through every door, but you will get into enough homes that you will be encouraged.

So press on. Someone will let you in to talk to him or her. This is also the reason that prayer for the Lord's direction is so vital.

DON'T BE DISCOURAGED OR INTIMIDATED.

> But God hath chosen the foolish things of the world
> to confound the wise;
> and God hath chosen the weak things of the world
> to confound the things which are mighty;
> (1 Cor. 1:27)
> I can do all things through Christ which
> strengtheneth me. (Phil. 4:13)

## Introductory Conversation

Now that you're inside, what do you do? The best thing is to start a conversation. Ask the person where they work. Do you know any of their relatives? How long have they lived in the community? Do they go to church anywhere? Is there an interesting object or picture in their living room? Ask about it. What's their favorite sports team? You need to do something to start the conversation and keep it going. A working knowledge of the community comes in very handy at a time like this. You should continue the conversation long enough to establish a rapport with the individual.

## Presenting the Plan of Salvation

Once you have broken the ice, you need to present the plan of salvation. It would probably be easier to go on talking all evening, but you need to stop at some point. To make the transition to the reason you are there, tell them you enjoyed the visit and appreciate their time. Then say,

# DOOR-TO-DOOR EVANGELISM

"As Christians we are concerned about some things and would like to ask you a question that only you can answer. There is one question that will quickly get to the point. Ask the person the following: "If you were to die right now, do you know for certain that you would go to heaven?" If the person answers yes, you need to ask them this follow-up question: "Could you tell me what you are depending on to get you to heaven?"

These two questions can open the door for you to witness. If they answer no to the first question or can't give you a correct answer to the second, then ask them this question: "Would you be willing to let me take just a few minutes to share with you from the Bible how you can know for sure that you will go to heaven when you die and never doubt it again?" After you have asked these questions, refer to chapter 22 for instructions on what to do next.

## Minimizing Distractions

While you are sharing the plan of salvation with someone, it is important to keep distractions to a minimum. One soul-winner can pray and amuse any young children in the home. He should do anything and everything he can to head off distractions, while his partner presents the plan of salvation. If the TV is on, you could ask if they could turn it down a little. Prayer before your visit is also important here. Satan is a master strategist when it comes to distractions. He wants to hinder the gospel message.

## Talking to Those Who Have Already Heard

When you ask: If you were to die right now, do you know for certain that you would go to heaven? You will get many varied answers. These include: "I hope I would," "I'm pretty sure I would," "I know I wouldn't," "I'm 90 percent sure," and "I would not." These are not people who have never heard of Jesus Christ. These are not people who don't know that Jesus died to pay their sin debt. These are not people who are not trusting in Christ. These are probably people who are only partially trusting Christ. They need to hear a clear presentation of the gospel and/or get the assurance of their salvation.

If I go into a house and ask the above question of a man with a beer in his hand and cigarettes in his shirt pocket and he says, "Yes I am 100 percent sure I will go to heaven because I am completely trusting Christ's death on the cross as my only hope for heaven," I would believe that this man is saved. Now if I go into another house, I might find a clean-cut man with Bible verses and pictures of Jesus on the wall and a well-worn KJV Bible on his coffee table. If I ask him the same question and he says, "I'm pretty sure," I would not have much confidence in his salvation. If I probed further and asked, "Well, what are you depending on to make you pretty sure," and he said, "Well, I try to keep the ten commandments and I'm a deacon in my church," then I would be almost certain he is not saved. The first man is saved but needs help cleaning up his life. The second man is not saved. You should tell him he can absolutely be sure that he's saved. Then show him how to trust in Jesus to the exclusion of other things.

Most Christians think that those who have heard the gospel have either accepted it or rejected it. The truth is many people have heard an incorrect or muddled message. More people in the United States are unsaved because of a wrong message than no message. Almost every unsaved person we present the gospel to already knows about the death, burial, and resurrection of Jesus Christ. Our job has been to get them to trust Christ exclusively so that salvation of their soul can take place. This means helping them identify and throw out all the other things they are also trusting. Never assume that because a person seems to be familiar with the gospel or they attend church regularly that they truly know Jesus as their Savior: Remember what it says in Matthew 7:21–23:

> Not every one that saith unto me, Lord, Lord, shall enter into the kingdom of heaven; but he that doeth the will of my Father which is in heaven. Many will say to me in that day, Lord, Lord, have we not prophesied in thy name? and in thy name have cast out devils? and in thy name done many wonderful works? And then will I profess unto them, I never knew you; depart from me, ye that work iniquity.

# CHAPTER 19
## ALTAR SALVATIONS

IT'S SUNDAY, IT'S 11:55 A.M. and we're listening to the end of the service at First Community Bible Church.

Pastor Jones: As the organist plays softly I want you to stand.
Please bow your heads.
Do you know Jesus as your personal Savior?
Have you made Him Lord of your life?
With no one looking around, have you confessed Christ publicly?
Have you given your heart to Jesus?
Please raise your hand if you have received Jesus as your personal Savior.
Please raise your hand if you have placed all of your faith in Jesus Christ.
Have you turned from all your sins?
Have you made a commitment to Christ?
Have you made a public profession of faith?

## CONFLICTING SIGNS CONFUSE SINNERS

> This morning I want you to surrender your life to Christ.
> I want you to confess all your sins to Him.
> If you're under conviction this morning I want you to invite Jesus in to your life.
> You need to repent and believe the gospel and follow Jesus by faith.
> You need to say the sinner's prayer.
> This morning if you haven't accepted, sorrowed, repented, surrendered, followed, received, turned, confessed, and believed, I want you to come forward.
> I don't want any hesitation.
> Come right now as we sing:

Song Leader:
> Just as I turn from all my sins.
> Let thy conviction fall on me.
> And I'll surrender my life to thee.
> Oh Lamb of God, I follow! I commit!
>
> Just as I make Jesus my Lord
> And all my heart to Him I give
> Because my sorrow I cannot bear
> Oh Lamb of God, I repent! I Believe!

Do you know where the worst location for someone to get saved is? It's the church altar. What? Why's that? I'm glad you asked. Many people feel the Holy Spirit urging them to make a decision and they walk an aisle, but how often do they know exactly what to do when they get to the altar?

As you can see from the exaggerated illustration above, pastors and preachers can sometimes be very unclear or even contradictory in what they ask the unsaved to do. Did the pastor mention that someone would be at the altar to talk to them individually? Has the church trained anyone to explain the plan of salvation to them and answer any questions

## ALTAR SALVATIONS

they might have? If someone tried to communicate with an individual at the altar, could they hear above the organ and invitational hymn? Does anyone feel personally responsible for discipleship after leading a person to Christ at the altar? Does anyone even know or remember the names of those saved at the altar? Maybe not. Often these people are led in a group prayer without asking each individual exactly why he or she is coming forward for the invitation. It is also difficult at the altar to assess a person's needs and to determine whether or not they understood the plan of salvation.

An altar service does not have to be this way. If you can get an individual into a private area, free from distraction after they have walked an aisle, then a lousy opportunity becomes a great one. Now you can determine the true nature of his or her need. You can then explain the plan of salvation, make certain they understand it, and answer any questions they might have.

After a person who has come to the altar has accepted Jesus as their Savior, it's important that you get their name, address, and phone number, if possible. It would be a very good idea to go and visit this person the next time your church has visitation. Make certain that at this point you again review the plan of salvation and their decision for Christ and help give them assurance of their salvation. Invite them back to church, and offer to give them a ride if they don't have transportation. Take personal responsibility for this convert. Don't assume that someone else will. Review the chapter on discipleship and make a sincere effort to disciple this individual. If you don't, this new convert will become easy prey for Satan. "Be sober, be vigilant; because your adversary the devil, as a roaring lion, walketh about, seeking whom he may devour" (1 Peter 5:8).

## CHAPTER 20
# HANDING OUT TRACTS

### Check the Message

Handing out tracts can be an effective method of witnessing, because you can give out tracts in many locations. Before we consider where to hand them out, let's look at the different types of tracts that are available.

There are a number of varieties of tracts you can pass out. Unfortunately, the vast majority emphasize turning from your sins or making Jesus Lord of your life. Most also give a number of steps that must be taken in order to obtain salvation. These often include confessing your sin, expressing sorrow for your sin, asking Jesus to forgive you, and repeating a sinner's prayer. If you have read thus far you are aware of the authors' objections to these additions to the plan of salvation. Please don't add any more confusion to the concept most people have about salvation by giving out tracts with an unclear message.

*No directions are better than wrong directions.*

## CONFLICTING SIGNS CONFUSE SINNERS

In order to make certain you don't perpetuate these problems, it is imperative that you read sample tracts before you order them. It is OK to be picky. You can view many sample tracts online. What should you look for? First of all the simpler they are, the better. Some tracts just contain scripture. These are often very good. Others have an orderly progression such as using the Romans Road with some commentary after each verse (see below). These are also good. There are many other good tracts available, but those with unclear messages far outnumber those with good messages. So make certain you find good tracts before you start passing them out or leaving them at locations like those suggested below.

The Romans Road:

| | |
|---|---|
| Everyone is a sinner | Romans 3:23 |
| Sinners owe a penalty | Romans 6:23 |
| Jesus paid the penalty | Romans 5:8 |
| Believe on Jesus | Romans 10:9-10 |

Many confusing messages can be found in tracts and from other media sources. Dr. Charles Ryrie has collected an extensive list.[1]

We do have some recommendation about tracts. One of the best is "How to Know You Are Going to Heaven" by Dr. Curtis Hutson. It is short, to the point, and accurate, containing no additions to the plan of salvation. Dr. Hutson has also written another tract, which is also very good but rather lengthy, entitled Salvation Plain and Simple[2]. Two good ways to use this tract would be to leave it with individuals who have been led to Christ, or with those who have had the plan of salvation explained to them.

# HANDING OUT TRACTS

While we don't fully subscribe to the message contained in Chick tracts[3] this author (Paul) believes they are helpful in many situation. First of all, they do get read. I have had students at school who would look every day to see if any Chick Tracts were displayed that they had not read. Chick Tracts are useful because they contain a great deal of scripture in a comic book format that appeals to both children and adults. The major drawback is their emphasis on turning from sins, as found on the back cover of each tract. Also, there are references to making Jesus Lord of one's life in some of the tracts. While they may have less than a perfect message, I still recommend them because of the tremendous appeal they have.

## CONFLICTING SIGNS CONFUSE SINNERS

Another outstanding source of tracts is Living Waters.[4] They offer many other tracts that really grab people's attention. A number of them look like real money. These tracts play upon people's greed for money and then lead them into a salvation presentation. Other tracts challenge people's intelligence. All of the tracts emphasize getting people to know that they are sinners before they recognize their need for salvation. One drawback, however, is that some of the tracts define repentance as turning from sin.

## Location, Location, Location

The following list contains some suggested locations where you could hand out tracts:

1. At the mall
2. On street corners
3. At work
4. At bus stops
5. In front of the grocery store
6. At school
7. On college campuses
8. At airports
9. In front of movie theaters
10. At flea markets
11. At the farmer's market
12. Door-to-door
13. At the playground
14. At the bus station
15. At the train station
16. To the cashier at the store
17. At motel and hotel desks

## HANDING OUT TRACTS

If you are in front of a business establishment or at the mall, check with the management to make certain they approve of what you are doing. Many stores have signs posted which prohibit loitering. Don't give Christians a bad reputation by violating the policy of the store.

Here are some additional ways and places you can distribute tracts:

1. When you pay your bills by mail
2. With your tip at a restaurant
3. In hotel/motel rooms
4. In elevators
5. At the laundromat
6. At the doctor's office on the magazine table
7. On top of newspaper dispensers
8. On top of ATM machines
9. In taxicabs
10. In public restrooms
11. On bare shelves in stores

# CHAPTER 21
# OTHER METHODS OF WITNESSING

WHILE GOING DOOR-TO-DOOR and passing out tracts are common methods of witnessing, there are many other possibilities that may work for you and your church.

## Outdoor Services

My church (Paul) has outdoor services in public places like housing projects. There we do activities to present the gospel. Activities include puppets, drama, games, and music. These are different from tent crusades because they are done in close proximity to where people live and depend largely on attention-getting activities to draw a crowd.

The advantages to this method are that it gives people from a church the opportunity to participate, and it allows strangers to feel more comfortable because there is already a crowd. The major disadvantage for outdoor services is that you must take chairs and portable sound equipment with you.

## Church Sponsored Activities

In some areas certain activities are more productive than other types of evangelism. We are not talking about church dinners here. I (Paul) am familiar with one church that has two activities that have reaped benefits in the salvation, discipleship, and church involvement of many individuals.

The first is an exercise class, which meets twice a week. Participants listen to Christian music while they exercise and hear a short devotional while they rest. This has proven to be highly effective. Individuals from the community attend because it helps motivate them to exercise. (Few people want to exercise alone.) When you get them to church, a perfect opportunity arises to give the gospel and share other biblical truths which will help them grow spiritually.

The second activity is for Mother's of Preschoolers. (MOPS—This is a national program.) This group meets one morning every other week. Meetings include Bible study and activities that will help mothers become better parents. This activity meets a need for those mothers who are at home with young children day after day.

If you are aware of a need in your community that can be met through activities like those listed above, you should pursue it. Never underestimate the evangelistic potential of any activity that will meet the need of the members of your community. Many people have been saved and added to the church because of the two activities described above.

## Recorded Messages

One novel method of evangelism is the use of a recorded phone message. This starts with an advertisement in the local paper. It would read something like this:

## OTHER METHODS OF WITNESSING

> HEAVEN, how to know you'll go.
> four minute recorded message. Call 000-0000.

Many individuals will respond to an ad such as this. You may also leave space at the end of the message for a person to leave their name and address, if they so desire. These individuals could then be sent some follow-up material. For an example of what to record, look at chapter 22: Presenting the Plan of Salvation. This gives a presentation of the gospel that was adopted from a recorded phone message.

He that winneth souls is wise.

(Prov. 11:30b)

## Salvation Key Chains

A salvation key chain is a gift item that can be used to explain the gospel. In order to make it you need a key ring, clear lace, and colored beads. Take a twelve-inch piece of lace. Loop it through the key ring. Tie a knot. Place six colored beads on the lace in order: black, black, orange, red, white, and gold. Tie a knot at the end of the six beads and trim the ends.

The different colored beads represent the parts of the plan of salvation:

Black: sin
Black: death
Orange: hell
Red: Jesus' blood
White: purity
Gold: heaven

# CONFLICTING SIGNS CONFUSE SINNERS

You can easily explain the plan of salvation by following the colors.

Black: Everyone has sinned.
Black: The penalty of sin is death.
Orange: If you die in your sins you will go to hell.
Red: Jesus died for our sins.
White: If we trust Jesus to save us, He will make us pure.
Gold: When we die we will go to heaven.

If you carry a salvation key chain with you it's likely that someone will notice the colored beads and ask about it. Then you have an opportunity to share the gospel. You can also make extras to pass out while you explain the plan of salvation.

## Lifestyle Evangelism

Lifestyle evangelism implies that the way one lives either helps get others saved or proves he or she is saved. Some believers, who never open their lips with the plan of salvation by grace through faith in Christ, think they are getting the gospel to unbelievers by their lifestyle. They may reason, "I'm going to win my co-workers to Christ by not going to the Christmas party where they all get drunk." That doesn't tell them anything. Some cult members might stay away from the party for the same reason. Matthew 5:16 says, "Let your light so shine before men, that they may see your good works, and glorify your Father which is in heaven." Does your light shine so brightly that your friends, neighbors, and co-workers notice? I hope so. Do your friends and co-workers know you're a Christian by your deeds, or do they just know that you have a big list of things you don't do?

## OTHER METHODS OF WITNESSING

To let your light shine on your good works is to enlighten others as to why you do good works. If left unenlightened, others may think you are working to get to heaven. This would not glorify your Father in heaven. You're not working to get yourself to heaven. Rather you should tell others that your good works are an effort to get others to heaven.

One of the good works you should do is to share the gospel. "How, then shall they call on him in whom they have not believed? and how shall they believe in him of whom they have not heard? and how shall they hear without a preacher?" (Rom. 10:14). Don't expect your lifestyle to get the job all done by itself. Let your lips play a supporting role.

# CHAPTER 22

# PRESENTING THE PLAN OF SALVATION

**You Can Do It!**

ANYBODY WHO HAS everlasting life should be able to tell anybody who doesn't how to get it. Unfortunately, many people put everlasting life and the abundant life into the same package. If a soul-winner doesn't draw a clear distinction between the two, they may feel unqualified to witness to others. To be sure, you can't take someone else further than you are yourself. But if you are a believer and you don't feel victorious in your own Christian life, you can still bring your friends and loved ones as far as you've come. You can still witness to them and keep them out of hell. God will use any believer to get others saved; so don't let Satan or anyone else tell you otherwise. The more you witness, the more likely you are to have victory in the areas of your life you are struggling with.

# CONFLICTING SIGNS CONFUSE SINNERS

## What Should I Say?

Here's a way for you to give the plan of salvation if you're not really sure of what to say or how to say it. This presentation was originally given over the phone as a recorded message, and it reads like a monologue. This format is given here on purpose. You will not be able to memorize this and present it as it stands. You should learn the basic principles and methods of presentation but never memorize it or present a scripted plan. It includes all of the essentials but leaves out all of the faulty ideas that many Christians frequently add. This presentation could be modified to suite your own taste or style, but don't add something that's incorrect. We trust you didn't read this far only to have you say, "This would be a great plan except it leaves out repentance and surrender."

## Monologue of the Plan of Salvation

Do you know for sure you are going to heaven when you die? That's the most important question you'll ever face.

So first, let's see what God says about where we stand. Do we all start off on the way to heaven then at some point in our lives we commit a certain amount of major sins and then our soul become lost and unsaved? No, that isn't the way it works. In God's Word, the Bible, it says that we do not become lost sinners, but rather we are born lost sinners. Romans 5:12 says, "Wherefore, as by one man sin entered into the world, and death by sin; and so that death passed upon all men, for that all have sinned." Now let's take a closer look at this verse. It says, "By one man sin entered into the world," or into mankind. That one man was Adam, the father of the human race. Adam sinned in the Garden of Eden and had to pay the penalty, which is death. As a result

## PRESENTING THE PLAN OF SALVATION

of Adam's sin, all born since Adam have been born sinners. Romans 5:19 says, "For as by one man's disobedience many were made sinners," Adam's disobedience made you a sinner at birth.

What is the penalty for being a sinner? Romans 6:23a says, "For the wages of sin is death." This means not only physical death but also spiritual death, as we see in Revelation 20:14. "And death and hell were cast into the lake of fire. This is the second death." Both of these are yours and mine, courtesy of Adam. It certainly looks as though your soul, the part of you that exists forever, is in a bad predicament.

But the story doesn't end here. The bright side to it is that you can do one thing to remove the punishment you deserve because of your sin. Someone else has already paid the penalty for you. In fact this person paid the penalty for everyone. Romans 5:8 says, "But God commendeth his love toward us, in that, while we were yet sinners, Christ died for us." Through His death we can have eternal life. First Corinthians 15:3 says, "For I delivered unto you first of all that which I also received, how that Christ died for our sins according to the scriptures."

Does this mean that you will automatically receive eternal life because Jesus died for our sins? No, it is not automatic. You must put your trust in Jesus Christ. Romans 10:9 says, "If thou shalt confess with thy mouth the Lord Jesus, and shalt believe in thine heart that God hath raised him from the dead, thou shalt be saved." According to this verse, you must believe if you want Jesus to take the penalty for your sin. Now lets look at the word *believe*. The word *believe* here means to trust. Believing with the heart means to completely trust. Halfhearted trust in Christ and half in something else will not work. Your complete trust must be in the payment for your sin that Christ made when He died

## CONFLICTING SIGNS CONFUSE SINNERS

on the cross. Many people are trusting in Christ halfway. You can't receive the free gift of eternal life (salvation) if you are trusting in Christ and also trusting in your own reformation or works. Now that you understand what it means to believe, confess now to Christ that your are completely trusting in Him for salvation.

Now let's review. Do you really believe that you are a sinner? Do you believe what the Bible says is true, that as a sinner you owe a penalty of death in hell? Do you believe that Jesus, God's Son, died to pay the penalty for you? Do you understand that to receive salvation from the penalty of sin, you must completely trust in Jesus Christ? If you can answer yes to all of these questions, then the only thing left is to tell Jesus right now that, as well as you know how, you are completely trusting in Him for your salvation. Now thank Jesus for the gift of salvation. Congratulations, you are now on your way to heaven!

Now let's see if you are really saved. John 3:36a says, "He that believeth on the Son (that's S-o-n, Son of God) hath everlasting life" (author's insertion). You are the person who believes on the Son. God says you have something. What did he say you have? God says you have everlasting life. Let me ask you something. How long does everlasting life last? Well, it lasts forever, doesn't it? When do you receive it? The very moment you believe. So, how do you know you have everlasting life? Because God says so, and He can't lie. If you died right now, where would you go, according to the Bible? If you have everlasting life, you'd go to heaven, wouldn't you? And how do you know you would? Because God's Word says so.

Soul salvation is not a process. It is a placement. Every saved soul is equally saved. Now, remember, you didn't sin or do anything but be born to be considered a lost sinner and you simply trusted Christ to become saved. You are permanently saved and cannot possibly sin or do anything else to become lost again.

Now that you are saved, you need to be conscious of any sin or disobedience toward God. In other words you want to get control of your life, or rather let Christ control your life. Your soul is saved because Christ did all the work, but now your life also needs to be saved or salvaged. This saving doesn't happen instantly like your soul salvation did. It is a gradual process because Christ uses you to do the work to whatever degree you are willing to let Him. Philippians 2:12b says, "Work out your own salvation." That's your life's salvation after Christ has already saved your soul. You see, you did contribute to your life's problems, and it has been in your own control. Therefore, the Bible says to work out your own salvation. Any positive and lasting change in your life will never be greater than your devotion to Christ. You can show this by studying scripture, praying, and attending church regularly. Christ will help you through these methods.

## Video Presentations

Living Waters Publications offers an excellent video presentation of the gospel.[1]

# PART 4

# STAYING THE COURSE

CHAPTER 23

# FRUIT INSPECTION

CONFLICTING SIGNS CONFUSE SINNERS

# The Spirituality Meter

(Helps to determine the level of other people's spirituality)

**Directions:** Give the person you are inspecting a score for each of the following questions. Then total up his or her points at the bottom and look at the key to determine his or her spirituality.

|  | Never | Sometimes | Always |
|---|---|---|---|
| 1. Does he/she speak to you at church? | 0 | 1 | 2 |
| 2. Does he/she sit near the front? | 0 | 1 | 2 |
| 3. Does the pastor ask him or her to pray? | 0 | 1 | 2 |
| 4. Does he/she carry a large Bible to services? | 0 | 1 | 2 |
| 5. Does he/she bring tasty dishes to potluck dinners? | 0 | 1 | 2 |
| 6. Does he/she remember to turn off his/her cell phone before services? | 0 | 1 | 2 |
| 7. Does he/she volunteer to take the nursery if needed? | 0 | 1 | 2 |

Total points: _____

## FRUIT INSPECTION

Key:

0–5: This individual is not very spiritual.

6–10: This individual is likely a big asset to your church.

11–14: This individual is probably the pastor's best friend.

WHILE THE ABOVE scale obviously does nothing to measure the spirituality of an individual, many Christians have their own scale for determining the probability of someone's salvation. This is often a scale that is based on their own lifestyles. If they don't have a problem with drinking, then no Christian should have a problem with drinking. If they don't have a problem with smoking, then no Christian should have a problem with smoking. If you don't measure up to this person's "Christian lifestyle," then you must not be saved. If you're a personal soul-winner, why don't you push the scale up a notch? Why don't you doubt the salvation of every believer who doesn't go soul-winning every week?

How do you identify a sinner? Is it possible to be a sinner and not show any outward sign? Yes, people with good character and morals are as much sinners in need of salvation as anyone else. It's not the fruits but rather the root that makes one a sinner. We are sinners because we inherited the sin nature from our parents whether we show many or few fruits of it.

How do you identify a saint? Is it possible to be a saint and not show any outward sign? Yes, people with bad character and morals are as much saved and on their way to heaven if they are trusting Christ as anyone else who is saved. This is because it's not the fruit but rather the root that makes one a saint. We are saints because we received the new nature when we trusted Christ. There are unsaved

## CONFLICTING SIGNS CONFUSE SINNERS

sinners with good character and high moral standards who might appear to be better Christians than saved persons who are not growing or producing fruit. These Christians have ignored or stifled the work of the Holy Spirit in their lives. We may have many fruits, a few fruits, or no outward fruits, but we are no less saved.

Does your salvation meter contain a nutritional clause? Most Christians living in the United States are under the

same veil of darkness that unbelievers are when it comes to good nutrition. Do you think it's a bad testimony for a believer to be seen eating a hamburger, a steak, or a large milkshake? Most people wouldn't. Only those who are enlightened about proper nutrition might see this as being negative. If they were fruit inspectors they might be tempted to say, "If that preacher were really saved, he wouldn't be damaging himself with that fast food burger."

If an unsaved person or another believer sees a Christian listening to rock music, what will they think? Will it taint the Christian's testimony? Probably, because not only do many Christians think that listening to rock music is wrong, but also most people know that Christians think it's wrong. Most people would not measure the likelihood of their salvation by their eating habits. Why should we measure it by their music preferences?

What type of fruits should we look for to prove the existence of a spiritual birth in an individual? Is it the absence of the fruits of sin? Is it an outward desire to attend church and read the Bible? We like to think that once a person is saved and the Holy Spirit has come in to live, that he will automatically begin to grow and bear fruit. If becoming a new creature means we automatically change outwardly, then there would have been no need for this passage in Colossians to be written:

> Mortify therefore your members which are upon the earth; fornication, uncleanness, inordinate affection, evil concupiscence, and covetousness, which is idolatry . . . But now ye also put off all these; anger, wrath, malice, blasphemy, filthy communication out of your mouth. Lie not one to another, seeing that ye have put off the old man with his deeds; And have put on the new man, which is renewed in knowledge after the image of him that created him: . . . Put on therefore, as the elect of God, holy and beloved, bowels of mercies, kindness, humbleness of mind, meekness, longsuffering.
> (Col. 3:5, 8–10,12)

We are told to put off certain behaviors and to put on others. Paul would not have written this if outward change were an automatic process.

The salvation of your soul doesn't clean up your life. God's Word does. When you trusted Christ, your soul was set free from the penalty of sin, but that is all the freedom that came automatically with salvation. In order for your life to begin to change and be cleaned up, it must be purged by the truths of the Word of God. If a new believer is an alcoholic, he may need to see twenty-five different scriptures on the dangers of alcohol. The greater the bondage a person is in, the greater the need for the Word. Giving up sins in your life doesn't come automatically just because you are saved. Neither does the knowledge that you must read the Bible in order to grow.

## Misguided Messages

When a preacher says from the pulpit, "If a man doesn't do so and so, I doubt if he is saved," Is he sinning by making this statement? Is it wrong to motivate believers to grow spiritually by telling them that you doubt their salvation if they don't love church, Bible study, prayer, etc.? This teaching implies that everyone who is saved is also surrendered. In some cases people even take it so far as to imply or teach that one must surrender his life in order to be saved.

Some preachers commonly say, "I believe if a man is saved he will live right, come to church, etc." That's like Moses saying, "I believe if a man is delivered from Egypt's bondage, he will enter the Promised Land." Yet we know only Joshua, Caleb, and those under the age of twenty at the time of the exodus from Egypt made it. The others were free from Egypt's bondage yet wandered in the wilderness. Many people who get saved and delivered from the penalty of sin never make it to the abundant Christian life.

Assurance of salvation is eroded when preachers make statements like those above. In order for a person to have true assurance about his or her salvation, it must come from the right place. If preachers were truly trusting the substitutionary death of Christ as their only hope for heaven

# FRUIT INSPECTION

and trusting God's promise of eternal life as their only true assurance of heaven, would they not teach their people by saying, "Look, if you are trusting Christ for salvation, you are saved"?

It is our observation that those who are warned to examine if they are really saved are not told to do so by asking themselves, "Am I trusting Jesus' death on the cross for my salvation?" If they are, then they are saved. This should constitute the basis for assurance of their salvation. If these individuals are still living a poor Christian life, then there must be some other reason for it other than not being saved. Those still wandering around in the wilderness can have as much assurance of being delivered from Egypt's bondage as those living in the Promised Land!

Now let's see what the Word has to say. In 1 John 5:13 we read: "These things have I written unto you that believe on the name of the son of God; that ye may know that ye have eternal life, and that ye may believe on the name of the son of God." This is how I know that I'm saved. It's because I believe on the name of the Son of God. You can't see my belief but you can see my love for the brethren. "By this shall all men know that ye are my disciples, if ye have love one to another." John 13:35 Love for the brethren isn't a measure of my salvation, it shows that I'm a disciple.

Those who point to one's bad behavior and try to use it to disprove that he is a believer, are taking liberties that the apostle Paul could have taken but didn't. The apostle Paul did *not* declare any of the carnal Christians in the Corinthian church to be unbelievers. He never said, "Ya'll better check up. If you were really saved you wouldn't be behaving like you are."

Why didn't Paul do what many preachers do today? Why didn't he tell the Corinthians to go back to the altar and really get saved? It's because a man's soul is saved by

## CONFLICTING SIGNS CONFUSE SINNERS

believing, not by behaving. If behavior changes don't follow believing, it doesn't disprove believing. Soul salvation is invisible to the human eye; it can't be measured by someone's behavior.

Paul heard reports of fornication among the Corinthian believers to a degree that had never even occurred among the Gentiles: that a man would have his father's wife. Why didn't he take the occasion to say, "This man couldn't be saved and do a thing like this? He needs to get saved, and many of the rest of you heathen need to get genuinely saved also for knowingly allowing this to go on." The apostle Paul never hinted nor implied that anyone in the Corinthian church lost his or her salvation, nor did he imply that anyone was never saved in the first place.

Is it possible for a man, immediately after he gets saved, to join a church, attend faithfully, teach a Sunday school class, win people to Christ, and tithe to then become un-surrendered to God? Is it possible for this same man to stop attending church, stop reading his Bible, and stop soul winning? Would this scenario indicate that the man might have never been saved in the first place? No, absolutely not. Somewhere this individual stopped following Christ. This is a very common problem in many churches and is by no means an indicator of a person's salvation.

If you agree that it is scripturally possible for a surrendered Christian to become un-surrendered after a period of a few years, then is it possible for a Christian to never surrender in the first place? Are there any Scriptures that indicate a man must surrender his life in order to be saved? We know of none. "For by grace are ye saved through faith: and that not of yourselves: it is the gift of God: Not of works, lest any man should boast" (Eph. 2:8–9).

FRUIT INSPECTION

## Lot's Example

David, Abraham, and Peter all backslid, but did Lot backslide? We don't think he did. Lot was saved and remained so. In 2 Peter 2:7–8 we read, "And delivered just Lot, vexed with the filthy conversation of the wicked: (For that righteous man dwelling among them, in seeing and hearing, vexed his righteous soul from day to day with their unlawful deeds)." How do we know that Lot was saved? This passage refers to Lot as both just and righteous.

Did Lot ever live a surrendered life? In Genesis 19:8 Lot offered his two virgin daughters to the men of the city for them to do as they wished. Also, Lot apparently did not have enough character to convince his sons-in-law or his married daughters to leave the city before God destroyed it. This does not sound like a man who lived a surrendered life. In fact, there is no indication anywhere that Lot lived a surrendered life. You can't slide back from where you've never been. Lot did not lose the surrendered life. He was neither a behaving believer nor a backslidden behaver. Lot was a member of that third and perhaps largest group of Christians: baby believers who remain unsurrendered for their entire lives.

# CHAPTER 24

## DISCIPLESHIP

### Teach New Converts to be Soul Winners.

WE HAVE STATED many times the importance of not making prerequisites to salvation. However, once an individual is saved it is important to disciple him or her. In Mark 1:17 Jesus said, "Follow me, and I will make you to become fishers of men." If we are going to follow Jesus, we must become fishers of men. If a new believer is going to follow Jesus, we should teach him how to become a fisher of men also. This is probably the most important thing we can do to help a new believer grow spiritually.

The reason it is important for a new believer to become a fisher of men is that he or she will be purged. Jesus said in John 15:1–2, "I am the true vine, and my Father is the husbandman. Every branch in me that beareth not fruit he taketh away: and every branch that beareth fruit, he purgeth it, that it may bring forth more fruit." A new believer will have his or her life changed by becoming a soul-winner.

## CONFLICTING SIGNS CONFUSE SINNERS

When you go out to witness to the lost, take a new believer with you.

In John 15:16 it says, "I have chosen you, and ordained you, that ye should go and bring forth fruit, and that your fruit should remain." The fruit of a Christian are the unsaved that he or she wins to Christ. The fruit that remains is fruit that reproduces itself. So we haven't done what we've been chosen and ordained to do until our fruit bears fruit. Remember that the apostle Paul wanted to go to Rome to have some fruit among them (win souls). (see Rom. 1:13.)

As you can see discipleship is teaching the new convert to win souls and staying or going with her until she does. Whatever other follow-up you do, it is secondary to this.

Proverbs 11:30 states, "The fruit of the righteous is a tree of life and he that winneth souls is wise." The fruit we bear is not what's on the tree. It is the tree plus whatever the tree produces. Our fruit is not the apple. It is what the apple grows into when its seeds are planted (discipled). In the true sense of the words "winneth souls," we haven't fully completed our mandate to Christ until those we've won to Christ are taught to win others to Christ. Discipleship is teaching the convert to win souls. First they are won from destruction. Then we win them to usefulness.

In Matthew 28:18b–20 Jesus gives us two more important things to do. "All power is given unto me in heaven and in earth. Go ye therefore, and teach all nations, baptizing them in the name of the Father, and of the Son, and of the Holy Ghost: Teaching them to observe all things whatsoever I have commanded you: and, lo, I am with you always, even unto the end of the world. Amen." First, we need to get new believers baptized; and second, we need to teach them to observe the same commandment found in Matthew 28 (going-teaching-baptizing-teaching). We are to continue doing this until the end of time.

DISCIPLESHIP

## Will God Use Unsanctified New Believers to Win Others?

The real reason living right or separated is important in soul-winning is that every act of sin costs the believer power with God. The less sin in the life of the believer, the more power he can have with God. The more Holy Spirit power he has, the more effective he will be in soul-winning. Jesus, our pattern, ministered not in His own power as the Son of God but in the power of the Holy Spirit. His love of righteousness and hatred of iniquity enabled Him to have the power of the Holy Spirit without measure. (see John 3:34; Heb. 1:7.) So, our own love of righteousness and hatred of iniquity determines how much of the power of the Holy Spirit we can have.

But we also know that the baby Christian who has nothing but imputed righteousness because he has just recently been saved should not be deterred from soul-winning. The woman at the well was a social outcast whose life was a reproach. Yet she had immediate results in soul-winning. That's because she had just become a believer and she was simply making other believers out of unbelievers.

You don't have to cross the Red Sea out of Egypt, then travel across the wilderness and cross the Jordan into Canaan to be able to help someone else get out of Egypt. Yes, God can use new believers as witnesses for Him.

## Here are some additional things you can do to help new believers grow spiritually:

1. Pray for them.
2. Encourage every new believer to make a public profession of faith. This will build assurance and

allow older believers to build relationships with new believers.
3. Encourage them to get baptized.
4. Develop relationships with them.
5. Call weekly.
6. Encourage them to attend church regularly.
7. Purchase a booklet written specifically for new believers.
8. Invite them to your home or take them out for lunch or dinner.

## CHAPTER 25

# THE BURNING BUILDING

YOU MAY FIND it difficult to assimilate all the information we have presented about salvation in this book in a single reading. The following analogy puts much of it into a unified perspective.

Imagine that when we are unsaved we are in a building that is on fire. The only way of escape is to jump out the window into the net the fire chief is holding below. The fire chief represents Jesus and the net represents salvation from the fire. The only way to be saved is to place all of your trust in Jesus and jump into the net He is holding below.

Many activities are going on in the building while the net is waiting below. People are rushing about trying to find a way to save themselves from the fire. Some brave souls are trying the stairs, even though they are smoke-filled. As they progress, they only find the smoke getting thicker. Those who want an easier ride are taking the elevator. They find that the lower it gets, the hotter it gets. Both groups eventually find themselves back on the upper floors unable

## CONFLICTING SIGNS CONFUSE SINNERS

to escape from the fire. They are weary for their efforts but no more saved from the fire than when they started.

Some folks are more ingenious than others. They realize it is a waste of time to try to get out of the building by the traditional routes. While others waste their time on the elevator and stairs, they have been busy devising other ways to escape the fire. They reason, *Why jump and take a risk when we can get down through our own efforts?* They assume that the only people who will jump are those that figure they would probably die anyhow and don't have anything to lose.

Those who stay behind try two different strategies. One group hastily gathers bed sheets to make a rope to let themselves down to the ground. They fail to realize that the distance is just too great. They can never make a rope long enough to reach all the way to the ground.

The teenagers are trying a different strategy. They enjoy living dangerously and aren't particularly afraid of heights. However, their faith in Jesus is nonexistent. In order to make it to the ground, they are fashioning a bungee cord from some synthetic materials they located in a closet. After completing their task, one brave soul attaches the bungee cord to his waist. With a great cry he jumps out the window into the great unknown below. The cord works fine. The only problem is that he is left dangling a considerable distance from the ground. Reluctantly, his friends pull him back up to the window and confront their shattered dreams as best they can.

There are some "rescue workers" who have come to the scene of the fire to try to save as many lives as possible. One worker advises a young man high above him with glazed eyes that before he can jump he needs to give up his drug problem. He says, "Go right now and flush those drugs down the toilet. Promise that you will never take any drugs again. Then you will be able to jump."

## THE BURNING BUILDING

A second "rescuer" is talking with a young child. He instructs her that if she is contemplating jumping that she needs to promise to faithfully attend fire-prevention classes, give 10 percent of her income to the volunteer fire department, and carry a fire fighting and prevention manual at all times. An elderly gentleman who is a true rescuer is all but drowned out by the other supposed rescuers. He is trying to convince a young woman that the only way out of the building is to jump into the net. He explains that no one has been able to save himself or herself by taking the stairs or using a bungee cord. He tells her to jump just as she is, without reservation, into the waiting net.

From this analogy it should be easy to see why there is so much distortion of the plan of salvation. Jumping into the net requires the least effort, but it is the most difficult way because it requires turning away from all the other methods and trusting completely in the fire chief holding the net. Many people are wasting time with their own efforts to get out of the burning building. In the end, all of their methods will fail, and those using them will perish. Many of those who eventually get saved will have wasted a great deal of effort trying to save themselves before they decide to jump.

It is worth noting that most of the rescue workers were of little help. All but one gave poor advice, which kept many people from getting saved, or at least delayed their salvation. It doesn't do any good to attach strings to jumping into the net. Those who preach and teach an unadulterated version of salvation will be most effective in saving individuals from the fire.

You should also notice that anyone who jumps into the net is permanently saved from the fire. It doesn't matter how committed they are to reading their fire prevention manual. They may never help anyone else get saved from the fire but they will never perish in the fire.

## CONFLICTING SIGNS CONFUSE SINNERS

The only way the fire chief can save you from the fire is by your complete trust in him. You can't save yourself from the fire and you can't help the fire chief save you because he is the only person on the ground holding a net.

What else are you trusting? Are you depending on the stairs, bed sheets, or a bungee cord? They won't work. Are you wasting your time trying to give up a bad habit before you jump? Don't bother, only Christ can help you overcome your sin. Incomplete trust in Christ is distrust. All other methods of salvation fail, and individuals who never jump into the net will perish in the fire.

Place all your trust in the great Fire Chief, and jump from the burning building before it's too late!

## CHAPTER 26

# WHAT ARE YOU GOING TO DO?

WHAT ARE YOU going to do now? You might think that this was a nice book. You might even think it was a really good book and pass it on to a friend. But it has no purpose unless it changes your life and you use it to change the lives of others.

Let's look at some possible scenarios. Ask yourself, "What would I do if I were confronted with one of these situations?"

### Scenario One

In the lobby of your church you observe a tract on salvation that emphasizes the importance of turning from sin in order to receive salvation.

I would . . .

a) Talk to the pastor about it.
b) Pray that God will give the people using the tracts wisdom.

# CONFLICTING SIGNS CONFUSE SINNERS

    c) Locate some tracts with a clearer message and use my own money to buy them for the church.
    d) Remove the tracts from the rack, throw them away, and place some extra money in the offering plate to make up for it.

## Scenario Two

A friend at church suggests to you that he doesn't think that one of the deacons is saved because he saw him enter a theater where an R-rated movie was playing.
I would . . .

    a) Change the subject.
    b) Defend the deacon.
    c) Tell my friend that he or she shouldn't judge others.
    d) Go talk to the deacon who is being accused.

## Scenario Three

Your Sunday school teacher gives a lesson where she states that unless you live right, you will lose your salvation.
I would . . .

    a) Talk to the teacher after class.
    b) Disagree with the teacher politely during class.
    c) Tell the Sunday school superintendent about the incorrect doctrine.
    d) Find a different Sunday school class to attend.

## Scenario Four

You are visiting a couple in their home who have just started attending your church. Your soul-winning partner explains to them that if they want to get saved, they must make Jesus Lord of their life.

I would . . .

a) Find a new soul-winning partner.
b) Ask my soul-winning partner to amuse the children while I corrected his or her error.
c) Talk to my soul-winning partner in the car about his misunderstanding, after we are finished visiting.
d) Pray silently that the Lord will do something to fix this situation.

Your answers to the questions above are very important. Will you actively try to correct misunderstandings about salvation or will you just let things continue on as they have been? It is our responsibility to make the gospel message clear.

> He that believeth on the Son hath everlasting life:
> and he that believeth not the Son shall not see life;
> but the wrath of God abideth on him.
> (John 3:36)

## Tell Us Your Story

Have conflicting signs confused you or someone you know? We would love to hear about it.

You may contact us at:

> Trent Thompson
> P.O. Box 2404
> Albemarle, NC 28002
> or
> conflictingsigns@yahoo.com.

# STUDY GUIDE

## Preface: So What's the Big Deal?

Review Questions:

1. What are some wrong teachings on salvation that have caused confusion for unbelievers and Christians?

2. What are some of the effects of wrong teaching on salvation?

Discussion Questions:

1. Do you think clear, correct teaching on salvation is important? Why or why not?

2. Can you describe a situation in which wrong teaching on salvation kept someone from salvation or caused someone to doubt his or her salvation?

# CONFLICTING SIGNS CONFUSE SINNERS

### Part 1: Wrong Routes to Salvation

## Wrong Route #1: Repent of Your Sins

Review Questions:

1. What does the word *repent* really mean?

2. What is the only thing a person should repent of to get saved?

3. Give an example of a false belief someone would need to repent of before he or she could get saved.

Discussion Questions:

1. What does it mean to turn from your sins?

2. Are there certain sins that you feel a person must give up in order to get saved?

3. Do you know of an individual a soul-winner wouldn't lead to Christ because the person refused to turn from their sin? How do you feel about this?

## Wrong Route #2: Confess Your Sins

Review Questions:

1. Who should confess their sins to God?

2. What is the purpose of confessing your sins?

3. What does an unbeliever need to do to receive salvation?

STUDY GUIDE

Discussion Questions:

1. Do you think it's a good idea to have an individual confess some of his or her sins while trusting Christ as Savior? Why or why not?

## Wrong Route #3: Give Up Your Bad Habits

Review Questions:

1. Will a particular sin prevent a person from accepting Christ as Savior? Why or why not?
2. What does a person have to give up in order to receive salvation?

Discussion Questions:

1. Do you believe that if an unsaved person has certain bad habits it will make it difficult to lead him to Christ?
2. What would you tell a person who feels she has no need of salvation because she doesn't drink, smoke, or dance?
3. What would you say to someone in your church who told you she thinks you are promoting sin, because you told an unsaved person that he didn't need to quit drinking so that he could get saved?
4. Do you think that it is easier to witness to the poor and needy rather than the wealthy? Do you think most evangelistic efforts should be directed towards the poor and needy?

## Wrong Route #4: Be Convicted of Your Sin

REVIEW QUESTIONS:

1. What type of conviction is necessary for salvation?

2. What effect did conviction have on the scribes and Pharisees in John chapter 8?

DISCUSSION QUESTIONS:

1. Does the conviction of sin play a role in your Christian life?

2. Do you know anyone who was convicted of his or her sin but did not get saved?

## Wrong Route #5: Sorrow for Your Sins

REVIEW QUESTIONS:

1. What is the meaning of the godly sorrow mentioned in 2 Corinthians 7:10?

2. Will sorrow for sins make Christ more willing to save you?

3. When you are saved, which of your sins are forgiven (meaning the penalty for them has been paid)?

DISCUSSION QUESTIONS:

1. What does it mean to be sorry for your sins?

2. Do you think it's helpful if a person sorrows for his or her sin before trusting in Christ as Savior?

## STUDY GUIDE

3. You would find much sorrow for sin at an alcoholic support group meeting. Does this necessarily motivate these individuals to trust in Christ?

## Wrong Route #6: Give Your Heart to Jesus

REVIEW QUESTIONS:

1. What scripture verse includes the words *salvation* and *heart*?
2. What does it really mean to believe with your heart?

DISCUSSION QUESTIONS:

1. What do you think people mean when they say, "Give your heart to Jesus"?
2. Can you think of a better phrase than "give your heart to Jesus" that will convey a correct understanding of salvation and contains the word *heart*.

## Wrong Route #7: Live It or Lose It

REVIEW QUESTIONS:

1. What do we mean by the phrase *live it or lose it*?
2. How are we saved?
3. What happens to Christians when they sin?
4. Why is there no sin in heaven?

# CONFLICTING SIGNS CONFUSE SINNERS

DISCUSSION QUESTIONS:

1. If a pastor continually tells his people that they will lose their salvation if they are in sin, what effect could this have on the congregation?
2. Is there any harm in believing you will lose your salvation if you don't live right?
3. What would you tell someone who says we make salvation too easy?

## Wrong Route #8: Keep the Faith

REVIEW QUESTIONS:

1. What do people mean when they use the phrase *keep the faith*?
2. What's the difference between a believer and a disciple?
3. Is it possible to enter by the narrow gate but walk on the broad road?

DISCUSSION QUESTIONS:

1. Do you see any similarities between the birthday present analogy and the way some people describe salvation?
2. Why do you think many people don't get saved if it's so easy?
3. What do you think someone means when he or she says, "I used to be saved"?

STUDY GUIDE

## Wrong Route #9: Make a Public Profession of Faith

REVIEW QUESTIONS:

1. Name one individual in the Bible who was described as being a secret disciple.

2. What consequences could there be for being a secret disciple?

3. In what way could we be rewarded if we were to publicly profess Christ, even if it cost us our life?

DISCUSSION QUESTIONS:

1. Has your child ever acted in such a way in public that you denied he was yours? Do you think this is the sense in which Jesus "denies" those who deny Him?

2. If you lived in Saudi Arabia would you recommend that all new converts make a public profession of faith? Would this just be for a home Bible study or should they let everyone know?

## Wrong Route #10: Pray Through

REVIEW QUESTIONS:

1. When people *pray through*, what evidence of salvation are they seeking?

2. What should be the evidence that we are saved?

DISCUSSION QUESTIONS:

1. Is it ever appropriate to plead with God as it occurs when someone prays through?

2. What harm could come from encouraging someone to pray through?

## Wrong Route #11: Make Jesus Lord of Your Life

REVIEW QUESTIONS:

1. Who is being asked to present their bodies as a living sacrifice in Romans 12:1?

2. What are the two types of salvation?

3. Who is responsible for each of the two types of salvation?

4. What two things are being described in John 10:9–10?

DISCUSSION QUESTIONS:

1. What are some of the prerequisites for salvation you have heard?

2. Many Christians may not have made Jesus Lord of several areas of their lives. Name some of these areas.

3. What do you think someone means when saying, "She really got saved"?

4. Have you ever observed anything that resembled sheep court?

STUDY GUIDE

## Wrong Route #12: Say the Sinner's Prayer

REVIEW QUESTIONS:

1. What is a sinner's prayer?

2. What are some reasons why reciting a sinner's prayer would not save a person?

DISCUSSION QUESTIONS:

1. Do you think it is scriptural to recite a sinner's prayer?

2. If a person sincerely prays a sinner's prayer to receive salvation, are there any components that you think are essential?

3. Have any of your ideas about salvation changed while reading the first section of this book? If so, describe the change.

PART 2: THE ONE WAY TO SALVATION

## Chapter 13: Understanding Salvation

REVIEW QUESTIONS:

1. What does it mean to be saved?

2. How does one get saved?

3. What will happen to a person who does not get saved?

## CONFLICTING SIGNS CONFUSE SINNERS

DISCUSSION QUESTIONS:

1. Do you think some people don't get saved because they don't understand salvation?
2. Did hearing a clear presentation of the plan of salvation have anything to do with your decision to trust Christ, or was it primarily based on other factors?
3. What could you do to clear up some of the confusion about salvation among both believers and unbelievers?

## Chapter 14: One Way to Heaven

REVIEW QUESTIONS:

1. Describe some common misconceptions about salvation.
2. What key word is used frequently in the Bible as the requirement for receiving salvation?
3. What do the narrow and broad gates symbolize?

DISCUSSION QUESTIONS:

1. Why do you think there are so many misconceptions about salvation?
2. Why do you think it's hard to get someone just to believe on Christ in order to receive salvation?
3. What activities might be included while a person is getting saved that won't detract from a proper understanding of salvation?

STUDY GUIDE

## Chapter 15: Assurance of Salvation

REVIEW QUESTIONS:

1. List some common reasons why people think they are saved.

2. How should an individual get assurance of his or her salvation?

DISCUSSION QUESTIONS:

1. Why do you think many people lack assurance of their salvation?

2. Do you think some people in your church think they're saved but are not? What do you think gives them false assurance?

PART 3: WINNING OTHERS TO CHRIST

## Chapter 16: Praying for the Lost

REVIEW QUESTIONS:

1. Why should we pray before we go witnessing?

2. List some things you could pray for before you go witnessing.

DISCUSSION QUESTIONS:

1. Do you think individuals will get saved by preaching the gospel only, without prayer?

2. How much time, if any, do you think should be devoted to praying for the power of the Holy Spirit?

3. Some people feel that those who are going to be saved will be, and those who are going to be lost will be, so its not really that important to pray. Do you think this line of reasoning is valid?

## Chapter 17: Motivation for Soul-Winning

REVIEW QUESTIONS:

1. How will witnessing to others affect your own life?
2. Give three reasons why we should witness to others.
3. What will be the eternal consequences for our efforts to spread the gospel?

DISCUSSION QUESTIONS:

1. Why do you think it's hard for most Christians to go soul-winning?
2. In John 15:2, what do you think the fruit represents?
3. Do you think Americans are so saturated with the gospel that's it pointless to witness?

## Chapter 18: Door-to-Door Evangelism

REVIEW QUESTIONS:

1. What should you avoid doing or saying that might prevent you from getting in the door to witness?
2. What question can you ask before you present the plan of salvation?

## STUDY GUIDE

3. How could you tell if someone has already heard the gospel but is not fully trusting in Christ?

DISCUSSION QUESTIONS:

1. How do you think the Lord will guide you to the people He wants you to share the gospel with?

2. How would you respond to a person who doesn't want to hear the gospel because he says Christians are a bunch of hypocrites?

3. What would you do if company comes while you are presenting the gospel to someone?

## Chapter 19: Altar Salvations

REVIEW QUESTIONS:

1. Why is the altar a poor location to lead someone to Christ?

2. What important steps should be taken after someone receives Christ at the altar?

DISCUSSION QUESTIONS:

1. Have you ever heard an invitation like the one in the introduction? Did a lot of people get "resaved"? What did you think of it?

2. What steps could a church take to limit distractions during an altar service?

3. Who should take responsibility to follow up on individuals who are saved at the altar? How could this be carried out?

## Chapter 20: Handing Out Tracts

REVIEW QUESTIONS:

1. What should you do before you purchase tracts?

2. What are some locations where you can hand out or leave tracts?

3. What are some places where you should not leave tracts? Why?

DISCUSSION QUESTIONS:

1. Do you think that the unsaved are ever confused or misled by the various statements made about salvation on tracts?

2. Can you think of any ways to follow up individuals saved through the use of tracts?

## Chapter 21: Other Methods of Witnessing

REVIEW QUESTIONS:

1. How can the gospel be presented over the phone?

2. What is a salvation key chain?

3. What is one difficulty with lifestyle evangelism?

DISCUSSION QUESTIONS:

1. Which of the methods discussed in this chapter do you believe to be the most effective? Why?

2. Is there an activity your church could sponsor that you think would help reach the lost?

## STUDY GUIDE

3. Do you know of anyone who has ever been won to Christ through lifestyle evangelism (without a verbal witness)?

## Chapter 22: Presenting the Plan of Salvation

REVIEW QUESTIONS:

1. What are the key points to the plan of salvation?

2. What is something that should not be included in the plan of salvation?

3. What is an objection to the gospel that you might hear? How would you respond to it?

DISCUSSION QUESTIONS:

1. What do you believe is the most important aspect of presenting the gospel?

2. What would you do if you were witnessing to a person who didn't think he could get saved because he is a drug addict?

3. Suppose you just witnessed to a couple that were living together and led them to Christ. They seem to be unaware that living together is a sin. Do you think it would be appropriate to show them what the Word says about fornication? How would you go about doing this?

4. Do you think that we will be judged for adding to the plan of salvation or do you think the Lord is just happy that we are out witnessing?

CONFLICTING SIGNS CONFUSE SINNERS

PART 4: STAYING ON COURSE

## Chapter 23: Fruit Inspection

REVIEW QUESTIONS:

1. What makes someone a sinner?
2. What is the purpose of Colossians 3:5–12?
3. Why do we believe Lot was saved?

DISCUSSION QUESTIONS:

1. Do you use a salvation meter? What makes you think a person is or isn't saved?
2. Why isn't the sin of gluttony talked about much in church? Could it be used as a spiritual barometer of any kind?
3. What do you believe is necessary to produce real fruit in a Christian's life?
4. How do we know if a church is really successful? How might God see it differently?

## Chapter 24: Discipleship

REVIEW QUESTIONS:

1. What is the most important aspect of discipleship for new believers?
2. What is the fruit of the righteous?

STUDY GUIDE

DISCUSSION QUESTIONS:

1. Why do you think so many new believers quit attending church and don't seem to grow spiritually?

2. What could be done to improve the spiritual growth of new believers?

## Chapter 25: The Burning Building

REVIEW QUESTIONS:

1. What is required of a person to be saved from the burning building?

2. Give three strategies that won't save a person from the fire.

DISCUSSION QUESTIONS:

1. Do you think it is reasonable to compare salvation with jumping from a burning building? Why or why not?

2. Several strategies were given by rescue workers that were unhelpful. Can you give a real life example that was unhelpful in getting someone saved.

## Chapter 26: What Are You Going to Do?

REVIEW QUESTIONS:

1. Where is a location that you might see or hear an incorrect presentation of salvation?

2. Give an example of a common mistake you might see or hear in a salvation presentation.

DISCUSSION QUESTIONS:

1. How would you correct the problem described about the error in the tracts in the church lobby?

2. Would you publicly or privately disagree with other members in your church who teach errors about the doctrine of salvation?

# NOTES

## Chapter 4

1. Henry Bosley Woolf, ed., *Webster's New Collegiate Dictionary* (Springfield, MA, G. & C. Merriam Co., 1973), 249.

## Chapter 5

1. Michael Agnes, ed., *Webster's New World Dictionary* (New York, NY, Pocket Books, 2003), 29.
2. Walter C. Kidney, ed., *Webster's 21st Century Dictionary* (Nashville, TN, Thomas Nelson, Inc. 1992), 13.

## Chapter 18

1. Charles Stanley, *Eternal Security: Can You Be Sure?* (Nashville, TN, Thomas Nelson Publishers, 1990), 106–130.

## Chapter 21

1. Charles Ryrie, *So Great Salvation: What it means to Believe in Jesus Christ* (Wheaton, IL, Victor Books, 1989), 23–24.
2. Tracts by Curtis Hutson can be ordered from: Sword of the Lord Publishers, P.O. Box 1099, Murfreesboro, TN 37133-1099 or from: www.swordofthelord.com.
3. Chick Tracts can be ordered from: Chick Publications, P.O. Box 3500, Ontario, CA 91761-1019 or from: www.chick.com.
4. You can order tracts and other witnessing materials from Living Waters Publications, P.O. Box 1172, Bellflower, CA 90707-9908 or from: www.livingwaters.com.

## Chapter 23

1. For a video presentation of the plan of salvation you go to www.livingwaters.com.

# GLOSSARY

Please note: The terms listed below are defined as used by the authors. In many cases these may differ from standard dictionary definitions or the definitions given to them by other Christians.

**abundant life.** The opportunity a Christian has to receive all of God's blessings for his or her life (i.e., finances, marriage, raising children, wisdom, etc.).

**altar.** The front part of a church near the pulpit where people often kneel and pray.

**application of salvation.** What the sinner does to receive the provision of salvation from Christ.

**assurance.** The certain knowledge that a person is saved.

**baby believer/baby Christian.** An individual who has recently been saved or someone who has been saved for a considerable length of time but has not grown spiritually.

# CONFLICTING SIGNS CONFUSE SINNERS

**backslide.** A term used to describe a person who used to lead a holy life after being saved but now has returned to a sinful lifestyle.

**bad habit.** A sin such as drinking, taking illegal drugs, adultery, etc.

**baptism.** A symbolic act in which a person is immersed in water to symbolize the death, burial, and resurrection of Jesus Christ.

**bear fruit.** Bringing others to Christ.

**believe.** To trust, depend, or fully rely on Jesus for salvation.

**believer.** A person who completely trusts in Jesus for salvation.

**branch.** A believer who should be attached to the vine (Jesus).

**broad gate.** A point of entry that accepts any possible belief. This does not lead to salvation.

**broad way.** A road that is contrary to Christian principles and will not give a Christian the abundant life.

**carnal Christian.** A believer in Christ who is not spiritual and therefore behaves like an unbeliever.

**chastisement of the believer.** The discipline of God in the life of a Christian, which could take many forms, such as problems at work, financial pressures, or reaping the consequences of one's own sin.

**Christian.** A person who trusts in Christ for salvation.

**Christian testimony.** The perception others have of a Christian, either good or bad.

**cleanse from sin.** A step beyond forgiveness, when God removes all of the evidence of one's sin.

**come to Christ.** The act of receiving salvation by trusting in Christ.

# GLOSSARY

**commitment to Christ.** A phrase used by many ministers with an unclear meaning, most likely they expect that an individual will be faithful in attending church, reading their Bible daily, etc.

**condemnation.** Suffering the eternal consequences of one's sins because of failure to trust in Jesus Christ as Savior from sin.

**confess Christ publicly.** When a person lets others know in a public setting that they are trusting Christ as their Savior.

**confess sins.** To tell God or another individual about the sins you have committed.

**conversion.** Outward evidence of an internal change in one's life.

**conviction.** The recognition that a person is a sinner.

**death.** When the physical body ceases to function.

**dirty vessel.** A Christian who does not lead a holy life but who could still be used by God.

**disciple.** A person who practices the teachings of Christ.

**discipleship.** The process of learning how to be a follower of Christ.

**doctrine.** A clear statement about what an individual or denomination believes the Bible says about a given topic such as salvation, baptism, the trinity, the rapture, etc.

**eternal death.** Spending eternity in hell because one refused to trust in Jesus, also known as the second death.

**eternal life.** Spending forever in heaven with Jesus because you believed in Him for salvation.

**eternal punishment.** Spending eternity in the lake of fire, the penalty that awaits everyone who refuses to trust in Jesus for salvation.

## CONFLICTING SIGNS CONFUSE SINNERS

**eternal security.** The knowledge that once you have trusted in Jesus for salvation you can never lose it.

**evangelism.** Telling others about the plan of salvation and encouraging them to trust in Jesus as their Savior.

**everlasting life.** Spending forever in heaven with Jesus because you trusted in Him for salvation.

**faith.** Trusting God.

**faith in Christ.** Trusting in Jesus' death, burial, and resurrection for salvation.

**false assurance.** The belief that a person is truly saved even through he or she is not.

**false-based assurance.** Someone who is truly saved but bases his or her assurance on an incorrect premise.

**false belief.** A doctrine that is not scripturally based.

**false believer.** A person who thinks he or she is saved but is not.

**fellowship.** Christians spending time together doing activities that will build each other up spiritually.

**fellowship with Christ.** A Christian spending time talking to God and reading the Bible.

**fire chief.** Jesus.

**follow Christ.** To pattern one's life after Christ's example.

**follow Jesus by faith.** An unclear term used in some salvation presentations, which implies that a person must follow Jesus to receive salvation.

**forgiveness.** Not continuing to hold anything against someone who has wronged you.

**fruit.** 1) evidence from a person's lifestyle that he or she is a believer in Christ. 2) Individuals won to Christ.

**fruit inspection.** The act of examining other people's lives in an effort to determine if they are true believers.

# GLOSSARY

**gate sheep.** A person who believes it is his or her job to determine who should come into the sheepfold and who should stay outside.

**give your heart to Jesus.** An unclear term often used in salvation presentations to children. This may imply surrendering your life to Christ.

**godly sorrow.** Conviction of sin that has brought about a change of mind.

**gospel.** The message of the death, burial, and resurrection of Jesus Christ for sinners.

**gospel-hardened.** The incorrect idea that the reason many people will not receive the gospel is because they have already rejected it.

**gospel-ignorant.** The state of most unsaved individuals who have never heard a clear presentation of the gospel.

**grace.** God the Father giving us what we don't deserve (salvation) because Jesus paid the penalty for it by dying for our sin.

**half-hearted belief.** Only partially trusting in Jesus for salvation.

**head-belief.** Giving mental assent to the provision of salvation but being unwilling to trust in Jesus for one's own personal salvation.

**heart.** A term used to describe full acceptance as opposed to only giving mental assent.

**heart-belief.** Trusting fully in Jesus as Savior.

**imputed righteousness.** God the Father sees and declares his children as righteous, because Jesus paid the penalty for their sin.

**invitation time.** A time at the end of many church services in which a person is given the opportunity to walk to the front to make a decision for salvation or for some other reason.

**invitational hymn.** A hymn sung during an invitation time.

**judgment.** The review of one's life that every individual will face after death.

**Judgment Seat of Christ.** When Jesus judges the works of the saved.

**justified.** God seeing believers as righteous because Jesus paid the price for their sin.

**keep the faith.** The idea that you must continue to follow the teachings of Jesus in order to keep your salvation.

**let your light shine.** Telling others you do good works because you're saved.

**lifestyle evangelism.** A believer whose only witness is to live a godly life in hopes that unbelievers will notice it and get saved.

**Lord.** The position Jesus occupies.

**Lord of life.** The act of giving Jesus complete control of every area of one's life.

**Lordship salvation.** The false doctrine which states that you must make Jesus the Lord of your life before He will save you.

**lost.** A person who is not trusting in Jesus for salvation.

**lost sheep.** A person who in not trusting in Jesus for salvation.

**lost sinner.** An unsaved person.

**maintain your salvation.** The false doctrine that once you are saved you must do something in order to keep it.

**make a U-turn.** A term used by many preachers in reference to salvation, it has two possible meanings: 1) you were living for the world; now live for Jesus, and 2) stop sinning.

## GLOSSARY

**MOPS** (Mothers of Preschoolers). A national church-sponsored program that ministers to mothers with preschool age children.

**narrow gate**. A description of salvation. The only way to enter it is by trusting completely in Christ.

**narrow way**. A description of the path to the abundant life, which is only received by following Christ and denial of self.

**natural man**. The condition of a man before salvation, who cannot understand or receive God's truth.

**new creature/new creation**. What we become when we are saved because we have a new nature.

**new nature**. The character that is received when a person is saved. This may manifest itself into new desires like living a godly life, reading the Word, etc.

**old man**. The sin nature the believer still has once he has trusted Christ and received a new nature.

**pasture**. Activities which promote spiritual growth, such as reading the Word, praying, and attending church.

**personal righteousness**. Living a holy life and doing good works.

**personal Savior**. Trusting in Jesus for oneself.

**power of the Holy Spirit**. Supernatural enablement to obey God and to accomplish God's work.

**productivity**. The method by which some churches measure their effectiveness. This may include counting the number of weekly salvations and baptisms.

**profession of faith**. When an individual tells others that he or she is totally depending on Jesus for salvation.

**provision of salvation**. Jesus died for our sins, was buried, and rose again from the dead to make salvation possible.

**public profession of faith.** This term most commonly is used to describe an individual who walks down an aisle at invitation time to show that he is either now trusting Christ as Savior or has recently done so.

**regeneration.** To return the spirit of man to the original state it had in the Garden of Eden.

**relationship with Christ.** What is established when you trust in Christ as Savior.

**remission of sins.** God pardoning the penalty for one's sins.

**repent/repentance.** To change one's mind about something.

**reward.** What a Christian will receive in heaven if he or she faithfully serves Jesus.

**righteous.** How God perceives a saved person.

**righteousness.** Godly actions by a righteous person.

**root.** What you believe; this determines the fruit in one's life.

**saint.** Any person who is saved.

**salvation.** What you have when you trust in Christ: salvation from eternal death and the gift of eternal life.

**salvation by faith.** Completely trusting in Jesus alone for salvation.

**salvation by works.** The incorrect idea that you can obtain salvation by going to church, tithing, teaching a Sunday School class, etc. Any attempt to gain salvation or acceptance by God other than by grace though faith in the substitutionary death of Christ.

**salvation construction.** The incorrect idea that salvation is a process that starts when you trust in Christ and continues until your death.

**salvation of the life.** The result of following the principles of God's Word for living in every area of one's life.

# GLOSSARY

**sanctification.** 1) The process by which a believer progressively lives a more holy life as a result of the dedication of one's life to God. 2) to set apart.

**saved.** Anyone who has trusted in Jesus to pay the penalty for his or her sin.

**second death.** The ultimate penalty for sin; spending eternity in hell.

**sheepfold.** A metaphor that pictures the position of salvation and security of all believers in Christ.

**sheep inspector.** A sheep who incorrectly believes he or she is in charge of the gate to the sheepfold.

**shepherd.** Jesus. He is the door of the sheepfold. He guards the sheep and leads them to pasture.

**sin.** Breaking God's commandments.

**sin debt.** The penalty for sinning; death and separation from God.

**sinner.** The position we were put in by Adam's sin and remain in until we trust Christ as Savior.

**sinner's prayer.** A prayer offered by someone who desires to be saved, often at the direction of a minister, soul-winner, or tract. This may incorrectly includes a desire to turn from a life of sin and a commitment to live for Jesus.

**sin's penalty.** Physical death followed by the second death, which is spending eternity in the lake of fire.

**sorrow for sins.** Expressing regret or remorse for the sins one has committed during one's life.

**soul.** We use this term to refer to a person's spirit, the part of a person that is in contact with God. Technically this is incorrect, but we do this because no one uses words like *spirit-winning*.

**soul-salvation.** The part of man that's saved when he trusts in Christ. This is really his spirit.

**soul-winning**. Telling others about the provision of salvation and encouraging them to fully trust in Christ as their Savior from sin.

**spirit**. The part of a person that is eternal and is in contact with God. We often substitute the word *soul* because it is in common usage, even though it is technically incorrect.

**spiritual birth**. A description of the time in a person's life when he or she trusts in Jesus for salvation.

**stop sinning**. An impossible mandate often placed on those who desire to be saved to completely eradicate sin from their lives.

**stray sheep**. A saved person who has stopped following the shepherd (Jesus).

**surrender your life**. To yield one's life completely to the Lordship of Jesus Christ. In the authors' opinion no one ever does or maintains this; one yields one's life in parts and often on a temporary basis.

**temporal life**. The time a person spends on the earth before he or she dies physically.

**tract**. A small pamphlet that describes the death, burial, and resurrection of Jesus and how to receive salvation.

**true assurance**. The knowledge that one is saved based on the correct evidence; that is, complete trust in Jesus as one's Savior.

**trust**. To completely depend on Jesus for salvation.

**trust Christ**. To completely depend on Christ for salvation.

**turn from sin(s)**. A term used by many ministers that has a variety of possible meanings. These include: 1) to stop sinning 2 ) to stop committing really *bad sins*.

**turn to God in saving faith**. An unclear phrase used by some in giving an invitation. The most likely interpretation is

# GLOSSARY

that in order to turn to God, you must turn away from something else.

**two Lords.** The idea that Jesus is Lord in two ways: first, one can acknowledge that He is the real Lord over creation. Second, one can make Him the Lord over one's life (i.e., finances, marriage, decisions, free time, etc.).

**two salvations.** In the first part of salvation, one's soul is saved (i.e., he or she will spend eternity in heaven). In the second part of salvation, one's life can be salvaged (i.e., marriage, finances, wayward children, etc.).

**unbelief.** Not trusting in Jesus as Savior.

**unbeliever.** A person who is not trusting in Jesus as Savior.

**unfruitful.** A Christian who does not win others to Christ.

**unsaved.** An individual who is not trusting in Jesus for his or her salvation.

**washing sins away.** The incorrect belief that one's sins can be removed by baptism.

**white throne judgment.** The place where unbelievers are judged for their sins.

**wholehearted belief.** Placing all of one's faith in Jesus for salvation.

**win souls to Christ.** Getting others to trust in Jesus as their Savior.

**witnessing.** Telling other people how to receive salvation.

**wolves dressed as sheep.** Unsaved individuals whose intent is to destroy the flock (true Christians) but have every appearance of being saved.

**works.** 1) Acts of righteousness done by a Christian. 2) Acts of righteousness done by an unsaved person in an effort to merit salvation.

www.ingramcontent.com/pod-product-compliance
Lightning Source LLC
Chambersburg PA
CBHW030316080526
44584CB00012B/584